BEYOND THE ORDINARY

BEYOND THE ORDINARY

Spirituality for Church Leaders

Ben Campbell Johnson *and* Andrew Dreitcer

WILLIAM B. EERDMANS PUBLISHING COMPANY
GRAND RAPIDS, MICHIGAN / CAMBRIDGE, U.K.

© 2001 Wm. B. Eerdmans Publishing Co.
255 Jefferson Ave. S.E., Grand Rapids, Michigan 49503 /
P.O. Box 163, Cambridge CB3 9PU U.K.

Printed in the United States of America

06 05 04 03 02 01   7 6 5 4 3 2 1

Library of Congress Cataloging-in-Publication Data

Johnson, Ben Campbell.
Beyond the ordinary: spirituality for church leaders /
Ben Campbell Johnson and Andrew Dreitcer.
p.   cm.
Includes bibliographical references.
ISBN 0-8028-4773-0 (pbk.: alk. paper)
1. Clergy — Religious life.   2. Spiritual formation.
3. Pastoral theology.   4. Spirituality.
I. Dreitcer, Andrew, 1957-   II. Title.

BV4011.6.J63   2001
248.8′92 — dc21
                                            00-067686

Unless otherwise noted, Scripture quotations are from the New Revised
Standard Version of the Bible, copyright © 1989 by the Division of
Christian Education of the National Council of the Churches of Christ
in the U.S.A., and used by permission.

www.eerdmans.com

CONTENTS

INTRODUCTION

O ver the past few decades, the notion of spirituality has not been easily embraced in mainline Protestant congregations. As much as any aspect of the church's life, spirituality has been misunderstood, misused, and resisted by both clerics and laity. For some, it has pointed to a self-righteously pious attitude that has often been repulsive; for others, it has suggested an individualistic — even narcissistic — disengagement from service in the world; and for still others, spirituality has simply been irrelevant.

Yet, at the changing of the centuries, strange phenomena have begun to appear. Members of our congregations have gone shopping for their own brand of spirituality in the Pentecostal and New Age marketplaces. Retreat houses run by Roman Catholics have been filled week after week, and conferences with the word "spirituality" in their titles draw more than a fair share of participants. These developments illustrate how important it is for mainline congregations and their leaders to wake up to the spiritual hunger around them.

In this new century, mainline congregations need to awaken to the Spirit and the immediate Presence of the Living God in their midst. Without inspired leadership, however, awakening seldom happens. An awakened congregation requires vital, dynamic, and spiritually sensitive leaders. So we believe one of the major tasks currently facing mainline congregations is the spiritual empowerment of leaders, both clergy and lay.

Our observation suggests that many ministers have had no formal training in spiritual formation, and as a consequence most lay leaders lack a mature awareness of the Spirit. Our intention here is to provide a text that both clergy and laity can use to erase the stereotypes of spirituality and develop more vital models and practices for the church today. To that end, we deal with both personal spiritual formation and the corporate spirituality of the congregation.

In the pages that follow, we want to introduce a faithful understanding and practice of the spiritual life to those who have not yet dipped into the Well that is Christian spirituality. And for those who have already tasted the waters and still thirst, we want to offer a way to dip even more deeply into the Well. With this purpose in mind, we have dealt with the issues surrounding a vital spirituality for changing times, the importance of prayer and mission being held in tension, and the crucial role of Scripture in the formation of our lives. We have also underscored the importance of vision, myth, and discernment in the spiritual life of the church. In all these ways we hope to help congregations stay on what we call "the cutting edge" of their own lives and the new initiatives of God in the world.

We imagine a pastor gathering several lay leaders to read, discuss, and act on the insights of each of these chapters. It may be, however, that a layperson will suggest a study of this book to his or her pastor. Whether initiated by clergy or laity, the study is urgent for the church today. To facilitate the study, we have included suggestions for reflection and discussion as well as journaling exercises to encourage both learning and growth. By engaging the text in these ways, the pastor-lay group can develop a core understanding of spirituality for their own lives and for that of the congregation. We have introduced spiritual practices like discernment and visioning that will enhance the spirituality of the congregation and help it to become an agent of transformation.

If this conversation between pastor and people can begin or continue in greater depth, our efforts will be richly rewarded. The church needs strong leadership inspired and directed by the Spirit of God.

We are grateful for all who have had a part in the writing of this book — our wives, mentors, colleagues, and students. And a special word of thanks to Rich Dietrich, who suggested the title, and Julie Johnson and Pam Cole, who enhanced the project. To all of you, thanks.

ANDY DREITCER *and* BEN JOHNSON

Chapter One

IN SEARCH OF A
VITAL SPIRITUALITY

What a strange and wonderful God we worship, who permits the shaking of the foundations of our culture and of our own lives, a shaking so severe that we find nowhere to turn but to God. Not in the triumph of victory, not in the sweet wine of success, and not in the exuberance of others' praise do we seek God. Rather, in the emptiness of earthly fulfillment, the aridity of parched souls, and the ceaseless longing for something that we cannot name, we search for the pathway that leads to our Ultimate Love.

The shaking and quaking and longing have become so pervasive that they touch almost everyone's life. "Spirituality," a word once reserved for zealots, monks, and the deeply pious, has now become more common on the street than in church. We need only to walk through a secular bookstore and let volumes on Christian spirituality, New Age spirituality, and Eastern mysticism bear witness to us of the hunger for knowledge of the Transcendent. Publishers report that books with the word "soul" in the title attract legions of readers. Recently several television series have been remarkably successful because they have dealt with spiritual and mystical themes. Conversations about spirituality have become more common than discussions of the stock market, and people reluctant to speak about church or religion seem to have no difficulty talking about spirituality.

While it may come as a surprise to many people outside the church, great hosts of us in the church feel the same quaking, share the same longing, and find ourselves also searching for more vital spirituality. One of our colleagues, George Telford, has written about the longing in our denomination:

> There is an evident yearning among Presbyterians for a life of faith which is newer, fresher, more vibrant. People are hungry and thirsty — aware that in our churches, our religious life, and certainly in our personal lives, there is an emptiness and a brokenness. There is underway a search for an authentic piety for our time. This desire is not confined to conservatives, traditional Pietists, or faddish New Agers. It is emerging among so-called liberals, who never want to turn away from their passion for peace and justice, but who are ready to seek again a recovery of formative Christian disciplines, biblically rooted, focused on Bible study, prayer, reflection on the context of their discipleship, issuing in more faithful forms of obedience.[1]

Christians are searching for "an authentic piety," Telford says. "Piety," a word that has fallen into disrepute and ill favor in recent years, actually points to what we have referred to as "spirituality." Though out of vogue today, "piety" sharpens the meaning of our quest. For Christians, true piety, true spirituality, refers to lived intimacy with God in Christ. Piety means devotion to the attitudes and practices that shape and flow from a life with God. These acts of devotion would include loving God with all of our heart, mind, and strength, and loving our neighbor as ourselves. And certainly they would suggest disciplines like worship, prayer, and deeds of justice and compassion. Spirituality not only encompasses attitudes of the heart and the practice of spiritual disciplines but also includes all the ways we live our lives before God.

Misunderstanding Spirituality

In spite of the spiritual hunger that many are experiencing today, and the breadth of their search for a life in the Spirit, there is still a good deal of misperception about the meaning of spirituality, both among the baptized and among those outside a formal confession of faith. Ministers

1. George Telford, *Monday Morning,* June 1991, p. 19.

2

themselves feel a hesitancy born of such misperception in their church members' reactions to the word "spirituality." These reactions probably describe the attitudes of many outside formal religion as well.

For example, most of us react negatively to a hypocritical spirituality. Hypocrites affirm high standards of religious behavior but often fail to live by them. They are too eager for others to observe the depth of their piety. Jesus said, "Beware of practicing your piety before others in order to be seen by them; for then you have no reward from your Father in heaven" (Matt. 6:1). He also advised against the hypocrites' practice of "sounding a trumpet" when giving alms, so that others would see and praise them. Jesus suggested that rather than displaying our benevolence, we should give in such a manner that our left hand does not know what our right hand is doing.

He made similar comments about keeping the practice of prayer secret:

> And whenever you pray, do not be like the hypocrites; for they love to stand and pray in the synagogues and at the street corners, so that they may be seen by others. Truly I tell you, they have received their reward. But whenever you pray, go into your room and shut the door and pray to your Father who is in secret; and your Father who sees in secret will reward you. When you are praying, do not heap up empty phrases as the Gentiles do; for they think that they will be heard because of their many words. (Matt. 6:5-7)

Most of us are afraid — and rightly so — of exhibitionistic spirituality that longs to be noticed and praised. We've seen too much of this displayed on television, and we've been nauseated by a spirituality made for audience consumption. Some of us have had friends who became infected with this display of devotion, and their practices made our illness worsen. But perhaps we have been most sickened when we have watched ourselves utter a word or make a gesture that was designed to attract a bit of attention. None of us can long endure this intentional piety, whether in ourselves or in others.

Our suspicion of spirituality also stems from our disgust with those persons who use it to escape responsibility. Those who practice escapist spirituality find a way to bend the rules, to blame others, or to twist an interpretation of a situation so that they are exempted from responsible behavior. A very clear example of this perversion of piety arose in response to the ministry of Jesus. Critics of his ministry raised questions about the practices of his disciples — specifically, not washing their hands in a ceremonial manner. Jesus responded with a bold confrontation of his own when he said,

> You have a fine way of rejecting the commandment of God in order to keep your tradition! For Moses said, "Honor your father and your mother"; and, "Whoever speaks evil of father or mother must surely die." But you say that if anyone tells father or mother, "Whatever support you might have had from me is Corban" (that is, an offering to God) — then you no longer permit doing anything for a father or mother, thus making void the word of God through your tradition that you have handed on. And you do many things like this. (Mark 7:9-13)

Don't we feel the same mistrust when we see a man work eighty hours a week and claim that it is for his family, when all the time his presence at home would accomplish much more than the extra money he earns? And don't we also despise hearing a person lament, "I was made this way, and I can't do anything about it"? Rejecting God's will in order to do one's own will was not something invented by the Pharisees. This veering away from God's will and seeking to claim our own will reaches far back into the human story and is buried deep within each of our psyches.

Spirituality has also been marred by a vast number of pretenders — persons presenting themselves as something they are not. To his followers Jesus said, "Beware of false prophets, who come to you in sheep's clothing but inwardly are ravenous wolves. You will know them by their fruits. Are grapes gathered from thorns, or figs from thistles?" (Matt. 7:15-16). Regrettably, pretenders have not disappeared from the church or from our religious gatherings.

In addition to all these reasons some of our own colleagues struggle with spirituality, we can add the substitution of prayer for work. Many of the so-called pious in the church willingly extol the virtues of prayer, but when it comes to serving in the homeless shelter or walking with the street people to protest the lack of public toilet facilities, they cannot be found. Some of our colleagues in seminary are tempted to believe that persons interested in spirituality are a bit soft intellectually. They fear that spiritually committed students substitute prayer for the hard work of academic studies. Our experience testifies to the fact that most seminary students (and the pastors they later become) can find time for almost anything except prayer — including lives full of study and service. When it comes to following Jesus, no excuse for delay is accepted. Remember the day when "another of his disciples said to him, 'Lord, first let me go and bury my father.' But Jesus said to him, 'Follow me, and let the dead bury their own dead'" (Matt. 8:21-22).

The issues with spirituality that concern most of us in the church are not recent perversions but rather precedents as old as humanity. As we have seen, Jesus encountered and dealt with all of these issues in his teaching and his exemplary life. When Jesus met hypocrisy, escapism, pretension, or the substitution of self-absorbed prayer for hard work, he appropriately prescribed a new type of behavior. But these misrepresentations of authentic piety have soured the search of many deeply dedicated persons and have served either as a barrier or as an excuse for their lack of profound interest in their relationship with a present, living God.

These two realities — the spiritual hunger of the masses and the suspicion of spirituality on the part of both church members and church leaders — place many leaders in a bind. Something within every serious leader, whether minister or layperson, knows that the yearning for the Spirit is a sign of the Presence of God at work, but this sign also evokes feelings of frustration and inadequacy, since many of them don't know how to respond to this yearning. In addition to the factors we have already mentioned, there are other — and perhaps greater — forces at work in the hearts of many church leaders that influence their response to spiritual hunger today.

Other Influential Forces

Perhaps the earliest and most enduring spiritual influence on the lives of all the baptized has been their role models. Quite unconsciously, today's Christians learned how to live the Christian life and to serve Christ from their unintentional mentors, primarily their pastors. Sadly, spirituality has not been the first item on the agenda of ministers of the past generation.

During the last few decades, the ministers of mainline congregations have presented themselves as guardians of the tradition, ordained therapists, cultural subversives, or managers of institutions. In none of these roles did the ministers or the chosen leadership of the church consider themselves to be men and women of God, companions on the way with Jesus Christ, or adventurers in the Spirit. In many instances, ministers of Jesus Christ and their baptized congregations seemed almost ashamed to be outwardly religious and expressive of the faith they represented. Ministers who have assumed these superficial roles have created congregations like themselves, both distant to and suspicious of a vocal, open spirituality.

Many current leaders who have been nurtured in this culture have absorbed its norms and values quite unconsciously. Their communal experiences and pastoral role models have given them few insights into and skills for helping the seekers of our generation find the pathway to an experience of God. When pastors and other leaders do not understand the searching questions and the deep hungers of another's soul, it is all too easy for them to label the seeker a fanatic or an escapist.

Having grown up in communities that did not nurture an intimate relationship with God and without role models in the pulpit who demonstrated the vital importance of the spiritual aspects of ministry, many leaders possess no memories of the centrality of spirituality in ministry. In many cases the time they spent in seminary did little to help them in this respect. They were trained in seminaries that placed little or no emphasis on their spiritual development. The curriculum was demanding in the study of Scripture, theology, church history, and pastoral care, but it lacked intentionality in forming ministers spiritually. So the women and men filling pulpits today do not shoulder all the blame for their struggles with spirituality.

The nominal brand of religion that shaped many believers in recent decades contributes heavily to the lack of spiritual depth in many congregations and pastors today. But pastors cannot place total responsibility for their superficial dealing with God at the feet of the congregation or their childhood minister or their seminary training. Surely those pastors who read the Bible and pray during worship every week have an opportunity to interact with God. And those laypersons who have been set apart to discern God's will for the church cannot place all the blame upon the rush of the times or the example of the minister. Are not both clergy and caring laypersons called to take care of their own souls? Still, the problem with spirituality persists. Few pastors and lay leaders would doubt the importance of prayer, reflection, spiritual reading, and regular retreats, but most would confess they are too busy or too bored to actually engage in these practices.

In spite of all the forces and influences that have made us suspicious of spirituality, in some ways ignorant of spirituality and resistant to dealing with our own depths, one stark reality challenges us to shift from a negative to a positive stance in our struggle: the breakdown of Western culture. This collapse of our culture, alternately labeled postmodern, post-denominational, secular, or pluralistic, has created much of the shaking and quaking in the lives of women and men in congregations today. We suggest that the tidal wave of spiritual hunger sweeping the nation may have as one of it sources the loss of old certitudes about God, the nation, the family, and the future. We believe that the cultural breakdown producing this great hunger, which expresses itself in spiritual cries for help, signals both an unprecedented challenge and an unparalleled opportunity for the church and its ministry. It offers us an opening to a deeper way of living with God.

Imagine what the church could become if only it were unshackled from old images associated with cultural dominance and if it adopted a stance of openness to the hungers of a new generation! Can you imagine what it might be like for ministers to lay down their old, negative struggles with spirituality and open themselves to the hard questions of a new generation? And what if elders in the church became discerners of the Spirit instead of managers of the church's business? Would we dare believe that God is in the shaking and quaking that calls leaders to a new way of perceiving themselves and their ministry?

A Spirituality for Today

A young minister who found himself in the grip of doubt and soul pain sought out his old mentor. He began the conversation with a point-blank question: "What am I going to do?"

His mentor, knowing that he needed to talk and quite unsure what to say at this point, asked him to explain what had happened.

Eagerly he began telling the story about the call he had accepted and what it had led to.

7

"I thought it was the will of God. I prayed. I asked for guidance, and it seemed like the right thing to do. All the doors were open, and what the search committee wanted for the church seemed to match my skills and sense of calling.

"I went to the church filled with excitement. They wanted the church to grow. They needed a new building, and they wanted me to provide leadership in growing the church and building a new building.

"Amazing things happened. In three years we had received over three hundred new members, and plans were completed to build the new sanctuary. I thought everything was wonderful.

"And then I got fired. While I was away on vacation, the elected officials got together, talked about my role and my leadership, and decided they didn't want me as a minister any longer. They terminated our relationship. They were fair in my severance but nevertheless indicated that I should leave promptly.

"The severance came about a year ago. I have a job at another church as an associate, but my pain has not lessened.

"I don't like to admit it, but I hate going to work. When I get up in the morning, I wish I had somewhere to go besides the church. I go to my office and often just sit there. I don't have the energy to do the work. Perhaps worst of all, many days I wonder if I believe all this stuff anymore.

"If God is so loving, where is God now? Why did God let this happen to me? Can I trust God to care for me, if this is what it gets me? I'd quit if I had anywhere else to go. Tell me, what should I do?"

His old mentor sat quietly for a long time with his eyes closed. After the silence had descended like a cloud over the two of them, he finally spoke. "I hear your pain and your cry for help. I don't in any way wish to minimize the anger and anguish you've felt throughout this ordeal. But I must say that I'm grateful you've had this disorienting experience."

"How can you say that?" the young minister asked.

"If you hadn't had this experience, you might have settled for being a handsome, successful, get-it-done sort of minister. You might have settled for managing the church, manipulating leaders, and selling religion to new prospects. You can never trust in these substitutes for authentic ministry. You have been driven so hard against the wall of your faith that you must decide if you believe in God, what you believe about God, and how you will relate to God. You can never be a flippant, hail-fellow-well-met, seeking the approval of the masses. You now know the goals you were pursuing are too low for a man sent by God.

"My dear young friend, don't you see in this calamity, this pain and disillusionment, the evident invitation of God? If you can't see it today, ponder this experience until you do!"

What the old mentor knew, and what his young friend was beginning to discover, is that pain is one of our best instructors. The mentor was perhaps recalling his own bouts with darkness, moments when it seemed too difficult to go on, moments when he wanted to walk away from the church, the faith, and all the pain connected with both. But he didn't. He stayed in the church, he clung to his sense of calling, and he followed his pain into the depths. Doubtless he recalled how his pain led him to explore his demons, name them, and face them one by one. Ever since that day he had been a different man.

In situations where a minister has failed to meet a church's expectations and church leaders have then made decisions that have disappointed and pained the minister, there is an invitation from God. Neither elders who cling to old ways nor pastors who force change at any cost are free of guilt. Perhaps there is a relationship with God that opens both parties to their spiritual depths and begins a significant transformation. The conflicting expectations of this congregation and their young minister could, through the work of the Spirit, lead both to a rich new place with God.

Somewhere between the darkness of the young man's pain and the unshakable confidence of the old mentor lies a spirituality that avoids the superficiality we all detest and embraces a relationship with God that steadies the soul and empowers it in times of upheaval. This spirituality consists of an intentional relationship with God that often feels more like hunger and questing than fullness and discovery. At the core of this spirituality, a yearning for God drives us to explore the dark corners of ourselves, to pull into the light all the "stuff" that we have carefully hidden for years. This deep desire draws us into the presence of Transcendent Holiness, not to say or do anything, but to gaze upon the One who has loved us with an everlasting love. Our encounters with God leave a tiny deposit of certitude that gives us confidence that the Other will be meeting us not only in moments of devotion but in the common experiences of an ordinary day. And, miraculously, we begin developing a confidence that God truly is in all things and that all things are parables of his Presence to be interpreted again and again in new and fresh ways.

As we envision the future spirituality of the church, we have chosen to focus on three dimensions of spirituality: the sacramental dimension, the activist dimension, and the mystical dimension. Each of these is expressed in its own way: through baptism into the community, through following Jesus, and through embodying the Presence.

Dimensions of Spirituality

Sacramental: Baptism into the Community

The sacrament of baptism provides the foundation for the spirituality of the pastor and also of the whole believing community. Baptism is that sacramental act which reminds Christians of God's invitation to all people. As a sign of God's loving invitation, it is the act by which all Christians enter into the Church of Jesus Christ. As a sacrament it transforms a common element like water into sacred water that mediates the grace of God. The waters of baptism point to death and resurrection with Christ, to the bridging of the great crevasse between humankind and God. And ultimately baptism signifies the gracious, forgiving nature of the Creator. Saint Paul provides us with a penetrating vision of baptism, a vision inexhaustible in its depths. To the Roman congregation he writes,

> Do you not know that all of us who have been baptized into Christ Jesus were baptized into his death? Therefore we have been buried with him by baptism into death, so that, just as Christ was raised from the dead by the glory of the Father, so we too might walk in newness of life. For if we have been united with him in a death like his, we will certainly be united with him in a resurrection like his. (Rom. 6:3-5)

If the sacrament of baptism lays the foundation for Christian spirituality, then spirituality must have a sacramental nature. By "sacrament" we mean a consecrated act that points to a reality beyond itself. Baptism in

10

this case points to believers' dying and rising with Christ — the old life with its habits of self-centeredness and destructive behavior has been crucified with Christ. From the divine standpoint, the life of disobedience is dead.

But the sacrament also points to Christ's resurrection. As a community we have been raised with Jesus. All who have been baptized participate in the resurrection of Jesus — crucified with him, buried with him, and risen with him. From the moment of our baptism, we believers participate in all that Christ has done for us, but we spend our whole lives appropriating its meaning. Perhaps that is the reason Andrew Purves suggests that "Spirituality . . . is a perspective on baptism." He says that baptism is "the declaration that we belong to God and that our identity is in Christ. It is the sign of new personhood, of having died and risen with Christ."[2]

The spirituality drawn from our waters of baptism has been marked by grace from the beginning. Just as babies receive the sacrament without knowing its meaning or doing anything to merit it, so believers receive the spirituality rooted in baptism in a similar way. Spirituality does not consist in merit received for practiced disciplines, nor is it a state earned by any other effort. It is always a gift of God.

Baptism also suggests the communal nature of our spirituality. When we are baptized into Christ, we are baptized into his community, the church. Through our participation in his body, we share in the life of all believers. As Saint Paul wrote to the Corinthian congregation,

> For just as the body is one and has many members, and all the members of the body, though many, are one body, so it is with Christ. For in the one Spirit we were all baptized into one body — Jews or Greeks, slaves or free — and we were all made to drink of one Spirit. . . . Now you are the body of Christ and individually members of it. (1 Cor. 12:12-13, 27)

Since we, as a community, are the body of Christ expressed in community, our spirituality is bound to this community; it arises in, is nurtured by, and expresses itself through the community.

2. Andrew Purves, *The Search for Compassion* (Louisville: Westminster John Knox Press, 1989), pp. 107-8.

Because our spirituality is rooted in the community, it can never become a solo venture. While spirituality is very personal, it is not private. There is no "Lone Ranger" spirituality. Individuals do pray, search, recognize the presence of Christ, and have transformative experiences in the Spirit, but all these aspects of spiritual development have their roots in the community of the baptized.

In our quest for a vital spirituality, we have tapped the theological depth of the sacrament of baptism for our source, a grounding that remains throughout the changing vicissitudes of life and the rise and fall of spiritual fervor. Yet an adequate spirituality requires more than the mark of God's invitation to all, more than the grace bestowed upon us in baptism. It requires our choice, our action, and our engagement in appropriating the full meaning of baptism. The model of baptized disciples following Jesus suggests the kind of participation we have in mind.

Activist: Following Jesus

The spirituality of "following Jesus" begins with a call, a call that is direct, confrontational, and challenging. Matthew records one version of Jesus' call to follow him:

> As he walked by the Sea of Galilee, he saw two brothers, Simon, who is called Peter, and Andrew his brother, casting a net into the sea — for they were fishermen. And he said to them, "Follow me, and I will make you fish for people." Immediately they left their nets and followed him. (Matt. 4:18-20)

There is good reason to believe that these two fishermen had been followers of John the Baptist. John had baptized them, and they had heard John testify that Jesus was the Son of God. They had even spent an afternoon with him getting answers to their questions. But there came a day when Jesus called them to follow him.

This personal confrontation is precisely what happens in our day as well. Christ comes into our lives and calls us to be disciples, calls us to appropriate the full meaning of our baptism, to embody it in our choices.

12

The call to follow him empowers us to begin living out the meaning of our baptism.

This call to follow Jesus may mean following him into the desert of temptation (Matt. 4:1), or following him into ministry to those in pain (Mark 1:25-26), or going with him up the mountain for an encounter with God (Mark 9:2-8). The call to follow Jesus today encompasses the breadth of human pain and the depth of human need. It gives birth to a spirituality of self-understanding and wholeness of self, to a spirituality of self-denial for the sake of the brother or sister in need, to a spirituality of action and engagement, and to a spirituality of personal and social responsibility.

Mystical: Embodying the Presence

In addition to the sacramental spirituality of baptism and the activist spirituality of following Jesus, we believe yet another dimension of spirituality informs a vital spirituality for today — an embodiment of the Presence. Jesus introduced this spirituality in his final hours with his disciples. He said to them, "I will not leave you orphaned; I am coming to you. In a little while the world will no longer see me, but you will see me; because I live, you also will live. On that day you will know that I am in my Father, and you in me, and I in you. They who have my commandments and keep them are those who love me; and those who love me will be loved by my Father, and I will love them and reveal myself to them" (John 14:18-21).

These promises of Jesus lead us into the mystical dimensions of Christianity, the venue in which we encounter mystery and wonderment. Jesus promised not to leave us as orphans and promised that he was coming to us. And he did come. He came in the Spirit at Pentecost; he has remained among us since that day; and he still comes to us in the world, in the community of faith, in creation, in our personal lives. From time to time, all of us who follow Jesus receive a visitation by the Presence. This manifestation of Christ in our lives shocks us, startles us, fills us with a sense of wonder and awe.

On the day of Christ's coming, an amazing transformation occurs. His Presence deposits within us a convictional knowledge about Jesus' relationship with his *Abba,* an assurance that Jesus is in union with God. But Christ promises more. We will have the same deep inner conviction

13

about our own relationship with God. That is, we will receive the deep assurance that through Christ, God is united with us — even us! For humans to be in so profound a relationship boggles the imagination.

In our faithful quest to follow him, Christ will recognize our love, and as we love Christ, we will be loved by the One who created us and sustains us. Within the bounds of this divine-human relationship of love, Christ will love us and continue to manifest himself to us. The realities of these promises overwhelm our small minds because we cannot comprehend so intimate a participation in the divine love of Christ and the all-embracing love of God. In our efforts to take in the depth and breadth of this communion, our imagination falters, like a once-hungry soul unable to finish a lavish feast. This embodiment of the Divine Presence adds yet another crucial dimension to a vital spirituality for Christian leaders today.

What then are we to say about this spirituality for leadership in a changing era? The spirituality we espouse has firm roots in the long tradition of the church, a tradition foreshadowed in the baptism of Jesus and in the practice of baptism in the early church. Baptism begets a spirituality that draws upon the graciousness of God for its life; it is not a relationship or lifestyle that can be self-generated. Neither can this spirituality grow in isolation. It must be grounded in a community. And this kind of spirituality is governed by the principle of death and resurrection — the death to the old and the embrace of the new as given to us by God.

While this may seem to be a spirituality that rests passively in sacramental grace, it is not: it is awakened and challenged by the call to follow Jesus. This "following" aspect of spirituality stimulates the will to choose and act. In its positive form, it leads to obedience, to keeping the commandments of Christ. Following Christ does not create merit but does position us to manifest Christ in the world. When we leave ourselves behind and go with Christ into the aridity of the desert, the pain and suffering of the marginalized, the darkness that encircles the cross, and the joy of the resurrection, this spirituality shines like a floodlight in a dark world.

The mystical dimensions of this spirituality provide an emphasis often omitted from the practices of mainline congregations. Christ's coming to us lies outside our control. Christ and God dwell in one another in ways that do not conform to standard ways of deriving truth and defining reality. Similarly, our way of knowing that Christ is in us and we are in

Christ lies outside the bounds of empirical, rational thought. Nevertheless, millions have testified to its reality. This spirituality continues to derive its substance and its energy from a loving response to Christ's invitation to keep his commandments to love. When we obey his commands, Christ will love us and continue to reveal himself to us.

After this exploration of the roots of an authentic and vital spirituality, what more can be said? A vital spirituality for today finds its grounding in Christian tradition, is celebrated in the sacraments, and expresses itself in Christ-shaped deeds. It is a spirituality that seeks to follow wherever the Spirit leads, and it openly embraces the Spirit and seeks the living Christ to dwell in us and manifest itself in all our actions. When we understand spirituality in this way, it lays to rest the fears and suspicions discussed at the outset of this chapter.

New Vision, New Power

A spirituality grounded in baptism, informed by the example of Jesus, and empowered by his living Presence will gush forth as spiritual power in the life and ministry of church leaders. We hesitate to use the term "power" because for some it can connote authority over others or the ability to force one's will upon others. But the power to which we point does not belong to leaders. Power in ministry comes from God; it is an energy that flows through us. If we claim it, hold it, and seek to use it for ourselves, we block its flow and distort its intentions.

This power from God is nothing less than the manifestation of the indwelling presence of Christ working through us. The more transparent we are to the Presence of God, the more fully the power of God flows through our thoughts, feelings, and activities, and the more authentically we minister.

In this way we come full circle: we spend time with God, our lives become more congruent with God's intention, the power flows through us to the lives of others, and our encounter with their pain, suffering, and celebration drives us back to God. In fact, as our encounter with God moves us again and again to encounter the passion of human experience, we meet the passion of Christ in human passion. Our lives become more and more attuned to God's Presence within us, around us, through us,

15

and beyond us. This circle of spirituality that links God and human experience has repeated itself throughout the church's ministry.

Do you see the stark contrast between professional leadership and a leadership of passion and vision? To heighten the contrast even more, let us look more closely at the nature of this power that flows through our lives.

The power that flows through ministry is a convictional power. When the Spirit flows through the words and actions of the baptized, they recognize a deep conviction within themselves that God is at work through their words and actions. This power also affects those who are the recipients of ministry. They also have a sense of power moving toward them, a power that persuades or identifies with them in a manner beyond any human capacity.

The power flowing through our relationships, which comes from the Presence within us, often works through us without our having the slightest knowledge of its activity. God uses what we say and do without our being aware of it. Every one of us longs to be a bearer of the Spirit, but we can do nothing to guarantee that the energy will come from above. No matter how much we leaders pray about visiting a person in the hospital or how long we work on a sermon, it is the power of the Spirit that energizes the act or the message. The secret activity of the Spirit never enters our consciousness, and perhaps we will do our most effective work for Christ without knowing it this side of eternity. Perhaps our conscious role will be to live in wonder, pointing toward the bit of God we have encountered and offering ourselves as companions on the way.

The power that flows through us is healing. This work of the Spirit may be intentional and formal, as it is when a leader visits a sick church member, anoints him or her with oil, lays on hands, and prays. Persons are often healed physically and emotionally through prayer. Or the healing may come unintentionally in an informal situation. For example, the Presence may flow through a conversation between laypersons that brings assurance and peace to a deeply troubled heart.

The power that manifests itself through the Body of Christ is also transformative. When the Spirit works through us, people see new visions, hope breaks into their lives, and a new sense of the meaning of their lives emerges through their relationship with us, whether we are pastors or lay leaders.

Do we not long for a church like this? Or do we fear it?

QUESTIONS FOR REFLECTION AND DISCUSSION

1. What have been your stereotypical notions of spirituality?
2. We have focused on three dimensions of spirituality that believers express in three ways: as members of the baptized community, as followers of Christ, and as embodiments of the Presence. How would you evaluate these? What would you add?
3. What is your attitude toward sharing the ministry of Christ with the world?
4. What have been your most significant encounters with God?

SUGGESTIONS FOR JOURNALING

1. List the experiences and influences leading to your realization of being called by Christ into ministry. Review these for a few minutes.
2. Write a paragraph describing the hopes you had for your leadership role when you were called to serve God in a designated ministry.
3. Construct a word list that describes where you are today. Use words like "happy," "tired," "fulfilled," "lonely," "expectant," "fearful," and so on. Keep in mind that you probably have a wide range of feelings about your experience.
4. Write a prayer that flows naturally out of this experience.

Chapter Two

THE SPIRITUALITY OF MINISTRY

A spirituality for leaders challenges ministers and lay leaders to discover the spiritual dimensions of ministry not only in the secret places of Bible study and prayer but also in the public roles of congregational care, preaching, and administration. And spirituality touches not only the whole mission of the church but also the larger society through the public life of its members.

For many, spirituality seems to be a synonym for the practice of certain spiritual disciplines and has little to do with tasks and personal engagement with others. In other words, spirituality focuses on the inner life with only a nod toward the larger mission of the church. But if the leaders are unwilling to settle into being monks or hermits, spirituality must include the public or outer practices as well as the private and inner ones. The responsibility for this renewal of the Spirit rests both upon the pastors and upon the leaders who discern God's call to the church.

No one has written more penetratingly about the integrity of ministry than Eugene Peterson. In his *Working the Angles,* a book destined to be a classic of pastoral spirituality, he identifies superficial ministers as shopkeepers. He explains, "The pastors of America have metamorphosed into a company of shopkeepers, and the shops they keep are churches. They are preoccupied with shopkeeper's concerns — how to keep the customers happy, how to lure customers away from competitors down the street, how to package the goods so that the customers will lay out more money."[1]

---

1. Eugene H. Peterson, *Working the Angles: The Shape of Pastoral Integrity* (Grand Rapids: William B. Eerdmans, 1987), p. 1.

This metaphor of shopkeeper points to the superficiality of many of us pastors. Pastors too often are concerned with the external aspects of ministry: the size of the budget, the number in attendance, and the number of new names they have added to the role. When the minister's gaze is fixed on these achievements, he (most of the time it is a he) not only shows a lack of spiritual depth but actually inhibits his own spiritual growth. For too long this model of ministry has dominated the practice of mainline pastors, often to the dismay of laity and sometimes, we fear, to their delight. If pastors are to escape this entrapment, they need the support and encouragement of lay leaders who do not always measure the church's success in terms of the bottom line.

These "shopkeeper" pastors have also been called Constantinian pastors.[2] Both appellations describe ministers whose lives are out of focus and whose practice of ministry falls short of helping people pay attention to God in their lives. Constantinian pastors exhibit certain characteristics in their ministry:

1. They fill a role and adopt an identity bestowed by ordination. As ordained ministers, they have been set apart. Their pastoral identity makes others perceive them as different from other baptized members of the church.
2. They have become individuals to whom all the members say, "Sorry, Pastor" when they utter a "hell" or a "damn."
3. They have received gifts and discounts. Because they have been underpaid, they have received free groceries, discounts at the stores, free tickets to the movies, and complimentary memberships at country clubs.
4. They have performed perfunctory services like offering prayers at the Rotary Club, the football game, and the PTA before these gatherings became secularized.
5. They function in the community to marry, bury, and baptize, to hold the hands of the dying, and to visit the influential members of the congregation.
6. They are looked upon as role models, which requires of them good

2. Loren B. Mead, *The Once and Future Church* (Washington D.C.: The Alban Institute, Inc., 1991), pp. 32-40.

marriages, well-behaved children, and setting good examples in their communities.

7. They preach so as not to disturb the peace of their congregations. They never see a contradiction in being a Christian, a good American, and a loyal citizen, and thus they serve to legitimate the political and social status quo.

8. They are administrators of all the programs of mercy — the offering of food, clothing, transportation, assistance to waylaid travelers, and so forth.

9. They have chosen ministry as a career because it offered respect and provided ways of doing good works in the community.

10. They minister with a shaky confidence in Scripture and seek to conceal the underbelly of the church in its hypocrisy, greed, lust for power, and spiritual powerlessness.

As a result, Constantinian pastors of "yesterday's church" not only have become disillusioned but are visionless, dry, and bone tired. For many, each day is a fight for survival. This rather disparaging profile is meant to offer not harsh condemnation but sympathetic compassion. These servants of God do not need judgment — they need hope.

A description of the laypeople in the Constantinian church provides the flip side of the coin. These are the kinds of members for whom Constantinian pastors are responsible. These members can be briefly characterized by the following traits:

1. They have been reared in the church — baptized, catechized, and confirmed.

2. They have attended church functions and learned the language of the faith.

3. They have accepted roles of responsibility in the church.

4. They give generously to support the church budget.

5. They know very little about the nature of the faith and its demands.

6. They feel awkward speaking about their faith to others, even fellow church members.

7. They import a business mentality into their leadership, keeping a keen eye on the bottom line — number of members, records of attendance, and money.

8. They often feel a hunger for "something more" from their leadership positions.
9. They generally support the views and desires of the minister.
10. They occasionally suffer moments of disillusionment.

The officers of the church who have come out of this impoverished background cannot be blamed for their spiritual illness. For the most part, they have done the best they could to respond to the pastoral leadership they have been given. But it seems impossible for spiritually impoverished pastors to call forth and equip healthy, growing lay leaders.

All official leaders of the church, both clergy and lay, need to be aware of the enormous pressure that social changes have placed upon them. Unfortunately, the laity of numerous churches have taken out their frustration over sagging membership and diminishing finances on pastors. In some instances, pastors, as a result of the pressure, have fallen into despair. These struggling men and women of God need support and encouragement, not expulsion and punishment. A healthy spirituality will provide help for both spiritual leaders and the membership as a whole.

The Spirituality of the Lines

As an antidote to the maladies described above, Peterson suggests that pastors need to learn to work the angles of ministry. He describes what he means in this metaphor drawn from trigonometry: "Most of what we see in a triangle is lines. The lines come in various proportions to each other but what determines the proportions and the shape of the whole are the angles. The visible lines of pastoral work are preaching, teaching, and administration. The small angles of this ministry are prayer, Scripture, and spiritual direction."[3]

We are in basic agreement with what Peterson says about the angles, how essential they are for shaping ministry and infusing it with a sense of the Presence of God. No doubt "working the angles" does transform the shopkeeper from a merchant hawking goods to a servant seeking the Good. Working the angles of prayer, Scripture, and spiritual direction

3. Peterson, *Working the Angles*, pp. 4-5.

would also draw the Constantinian pastor from the external practices that flow from a privileged position to the core commitments of ministry.

Practicing the disciplines of prayer, reading Scripture, and giving and receiving spiritual direction postures the Christian leader to receive the presence of God. As God's light shines within and through the follower of Christ, ministry takes on a decidedly different hue. The church has always believed that the leader's relationship with God has a profound influence upon the practice of ministry. And Peterson seeks to help us recover the disciplines that make the transformation of this relationship possible.

Peterson warns that the lines don't work unless the angles are given proper attention. We would like to take this idea one step further by emphasizing that spiritually nourishing experiences and encounters with God occur not only in the angles but also along the lines, in the practice of teaching, preaching, administration, and — we would add — congregational care.

Those who labor in the faith spend most of their time along the lines, and if walking the lines always drains them of spiritual energy, they are destined for eventual emptiness and burnout. But surely God can be found in the lines. Don't we encounter the Presence of God in the practice of ministry? A spirituality adequate for a period of cultural transition must surely help us find God in the public aspects of ministry. For it is in the arena of daily ministry that the passions of human life appear. It is along these lines that we encounter the passion of Christ alive among us.

Not only do we spend most of our time along the lines of ministry, but the lines define where ministry takes place. A spirituality that does not arise in and flow through acts of compassion and justice cannot meet the demands of leaders caught in this cultural transition at the dawn of the twenty-first century.

Furthermore, it is along the lines — preaching and teaching and administering — that our worldview shapes our work and grounds our spirituality. Our Christian teaching and preaching point to a God who created the world, a God who came among us in Christ and brought us back to Godself, and a God who in the Spirit abides in our midst always. Our faith demands a God-inhabited world.

The worldview that shapes our teaching and preaching also informs our decisions. Because Christ is among us in the Spirit, we believe that through him God still guides the church in its mission to the world. Our task is to listen and to discern what the Spirit is saying to the church.

These aspects of ministry along the lines express our spirituality and also provide a source for nurturing it. But what are the signs of a spirituality along the lines? How is it discovered? It seems to us that the lay leaders of the church might see two opportunities in the situation to which we are pointing. First, they can affirm with their minister the spirituality of both contemplation and action. That is, they can encourage contemplation *in* action. Second, they can begin to seek in their lives a unity of their personal faith and their ministry in the world. In doing so they will have as great a need for prayer, Scripture, and guidance as ordained ministers do.

What are the underlying features that might help us discern the spirituality along the lines? Let's begin to identify them by taking a look at the caring line.

The Caring Line

An old saint of the church discovered that he had cancer. Hearing the sad news, the pastor went to visit him. Over the next few weeks the pastor's regular visits meant much to the longtime member and to the pastor. On the third visit the pastor began the conversation with a frank question: "Willie, I'm sorry to hear that the physicians think your cancer is terminal. How are you dealing with that fact?"

"Pastor," Willie responded, "you know how I am about those sorts of things. I have always lived a day at a time and trusted my life to God. If this is the next challenge for me to deal with, I'm ready."

"What are some of the things that you've been thinking about since you learned about the cancer?"

"I'm glad you asked about that. I think that often you pastors tend to shy away from the hard realities, perhaps thinking that it might disturb us lay folk. But now let me get to your question. I've been thinking about how wonderful life is. Somehow it's hard to see the wonder of life until you're faced with the specter of losing it. Life is so wonderful. And I've been thinking about how grateful I am for the life I've had. My life hasn't been perfect, but it has surely been good, and I am thankful."

"Anything else on your mind that you want to talk about?"

"Well, yes, there is. I asked the doctor to be honest with me about the surgery. He told me that there was nothing they could do for me, so they sewed me back up. I probably have from three to six months to live. I'd like you to know that I'm not afraid to die. I faced up to that reality a good while back, and I'm prepared in soul and in spirit for the next stage, whatever that may be."

"You know, Willie, the last time I was here, I felt you had something to tell me, but I didn't get the message. Is that true?"

"Yes — yes it is. I wanted to tell you that somewhere we got it all wrong. God is not an angry tyrant who has to be placated by the death of his Son. God is Unconditional Love, and Jesus died to show us the depth of this love for every one of us."

"And for you, this means . . . ?"

"His love frees us to become the persons we were created to be, without fear and without judgment. Life is so great. It has been a gift for which I am grateful."

Confident that the visit should come to a close, the pastor said, "I'd like to pray with you and the family before I go, if that's all right with you."

"We would certainly appreciate that," said Willie.

Instead of simply bowing his head, the pastor slipped over to the couch where the parishioner was sitting, knelt before him, placed his arms around him, and prayed. The pastor thanked God for the life of the saint, his family, and his contribution to so many people. The pastor also offered a prayer for the family. After the amen, all sat silently for several minutes.

The pastor arose, but before departing he said, "You'll never know what you have meant to me in my life. You have been a witness and a constant source of strength for me. I don't know how I would have made it without you."

And the saint responded, "You have meant the same to me. So many times in your sermons, your prayers, and your visits, I've felt the presence of God. You have indeed been my minister."

In this work along the line of caring, the pastor received nurture while giving it. This pastor also had received reports from numerous church members that they too had been given new strength through Willie's testimony.

The Preaching and Teaching Lines

A profound spirituality can develop along the lines of preaching and teaching. When teaching and preaching in the Spirit occur, everyone involved is energized.

When Henri Nouwen — one of the twentieth century's most profound spiritual teachers and guides — was a professor at Yale Divinity School, he held a prayer service at five in the afternoon every day in the small prayer chapel under the main chapel. One of the individuals who attended those services describes how Henri's homiletical teaching seemed to be a time of spiritual formation not only for those who listened but also for Henri himself:

> There in a circle of dim light, surrounded by candles, five to ten of us gathered, as we did every day, with Henri in an intimate time of simple singing, spoken and silent prayer, and Eucharist. At the heart of the service, Henri read one of the lectionary texts of the day and, after some minutes of silence, interpreted the Word for us. As always, he remained seated, his hands, voice, and face animated by the power of the Spirit he knew was present. Those who listened marveled at what issued forth from him.
>
> They knew that in that day Henri had neither prayed with nor studied that passage before those moments. Yet he drew from the text the heart of what his hearers needed. How could Henri offer such profound insights with such little preparation? Granted, Henri had a rare gift, but could we, as future preachers and teachers, taste the fruit Henri did?
>
> Since those days, many of his students have continued to ponder these questions. Over time it seems evident that Henri could offer us the depths of the biblical passages because he entered them so deeply himself. In those moments before he spoke to us, he did not simply ask himself what the text was about, he did not merely ponder what information it presented or what it meant. No, he *entered* the passage as if he were taking a journey.
>
> He poured his life into that passage, letting it pour over and through him in return. Perhaps he imagined himself there with Jesus, conversing about his innermost joys and anxieties. Perhaps he

was bringing the cares of the world for Paul's consideration, asking for the apostle's wisdom and understanding. Perhaps he was prophesying with Isaiah, embracing God's pain and the pain of God's people. Perhaps he was the serpent watching Eve walking in the garden, considering the frailties of this creature God had created. For Henri, a biblical passage was not simply a text for him to understand and teach, but divine, creative Word, a bottomless well that endlessly offered an encounter with God's grace, healing, justice, invitation, mercy, and love. And when he preached to us, he, himself, was being re-created by the Word.

Those of us who preach and teach need to learn from Henri Nouwen's example. We need to offer ourselves to Scripture as if we were on a retreat with it. We cannot set ourselves above and apart from it, focusing on our role as the expert interpreter. Instead, we must learn to approach the passage with the pains and joys of our own life. In fact, if we have embraced the people we serve, our life will be sharing their sorrows and celebrations. As we bring ourselves into the Word, we will discover that it nurtures us and spiritually forms us. And from our own re-creating encounter with God, we will be able to help those who hear to discover God's Presence in their own lives.

The Administration Line

The meeting of the church leaders seemed to be getting shorter and shorter each month. It was only nine-thirty in the evening, and already elder Paul Anderson sat at home, talking with his wife Claire about the events of the day, including the elders' meeting.

Claire went into the kitchen to prepare coffee, and Paul began to relax and review the evening's meeting. The group of fifteen elders had gathered a few minutes before 8:00 P.M. After a time of fellowship, Paul, as acting chair of the meeting, called the group to order. An elder who had been appointed the month before read Scripture and offered prayer. This elder asked the group to sit together quietly for a quarter-hour to attune themselves to the Presence of God.

After the silence, the coordinators of various task forces reported on the ministry of their group since the last meeting. Some really astounding things had been happening through the members of St. Andrews Church. One task force had responded to single parents in the neighborhood and had provided food, financial help, tutoring for kids who were falling behind in their class assignments, and companionship for lonely mothers. Another ministry had formed to support the widows in the community. On this particular evening, the coordinator reported on the group's efforts to get a reduction in the cost of gas and electricity for widows as well as elderly couples. The task force on outreach presented preliminary plans for a new ministry to persons from eighteen to thirty years of age. The lay leader asked the group to pray with him and his committee because, if the church intended to reach this group, changes would have to be made or new forms of ministry developed.

There were other reports on ministry, both within the body of Christ and beyond it. After the final report was given, the elders joined in a prayer of thanksgiving for God's blessings on their ministries.

Jonathan Martin had requested a slot on the agenda to share with the elders his sense of a call to a new ministry. He gave a short report on his awareness of the spiritual hunger of the new members in church. He related how a number of them had engaged him in conversation about what it meant to know God. Others had spoken to him about issues of discernment. Quite a few wanted to know how they could pray for him meaningfully. The minister had amplified Jon's statements with reports of additional spiritual needs in the congregation. Several other elders spoke of their experiences with members who felt something was missing from their life.

After a sensitive discussion of this need within the congregation, Jonathan indicated that he was trying to discern if God was calling him to begin a ministry to these searching individuals. Questions arose about inviting this group to attend church school, participate in existing Bible-study groups, and attend the contemporary service, but no one was particularly negative about Jonathan's beginning a new ministry.

When the discussion ended, the presiding elder asked the group to enter into silence and to wait before God. The group listened with Jonathan for the leading of God's Spirit. When the silence and prayers ended, no one had a special sense of discernment. All the elders agreed to pray with Jonathan for the next month. Together they would seek to discern the guidance of God.

The elders were dismissed with prayer, and all were home by 9:30 P.M.

As Paul Anderson reviewed this meeting, he couldn't avoid contrasting it with his first experience attending the elders' meeting at St. Andrews. That first meeting had lasted for three-and-a-half hours. It seemed the elders had argued about everything. Should Mrs. Zaprowski be allowed to park her car in a visitor's slot? Should the thermostat be set at 68 or 72 degrees? Would it be better to buy toilet paper by the roll or by the case? Whatever the issue, each elder had a notion about how it should be handled, and most of the issues seemed distant to the central task of the church.

To work the lines of ministry requires pastors who have a deep sense of the Presence of Christ and lay leaders who have both spiritual maturity and discernment. Tragically, the Constantinian church often lacks both.

Clues to a Spirituality of the Lines

If we are to find our spirituality enhanced along the lines, if both clergy and laity do indeed meet God along the lines of ministry, what are the clues that help us identify the Divine Presence?

The principle of giving and receiving along the lines of ministry may provide one of the clues to the Divine Presence. Most of us discovered early on that ministry is not a one-way street. A ministry to someone in need most often becomes a ministry to the caregiver. We may have visited a person in dire straits, but when the visit ended, we realized that we received more than we gave. In the pastor's visit with Willie, the old saint, surely he both gave and received. Who could look into the eyes of a man filled with confidence in the face of death without being strengthened in faith?

Or who could have attended one of Henri Nouwen's worship services without recognizing that Henri was both giving and receiving? Certainly those who attended were receiving an awareness of the Spirit's ministry through him. But perhaps they were also giving to him through their prayerful attention.

When a leader in the church observes the Spirit activating gifts, granting discernment, and creating unity among the people of God, she knows that she is not alone in the tasks of ministry. More than that, she

28

knows that God's friendship and blessing are hers through guiding a congregation in the Spirit. Like elder Paul Anderson, she can recall other days when leadership was splintered and the elders focused on peripheral issues. But through the ministry of the Spirit, the situation has been transformed from one of dutiful work to one of worshipful work.

In most of her public ministry as pastor, she gives care, inspiration, and guidance, but upon reflection she may discover that she also receives. The caring that she gives also nurtures her own soul. Indeed, what minister has not been enriched through deep, personal encounters with members of the congregation?

And, just as the minister recognizes the presence of the Spirit in the work of ministry, those lay members who serve others also sense Christ working through their efforts. The spirituality of "yesterday's church" makes it difficult to talk about Christ in these ordinary situations. It sounds too pious to speak of Christ, even though his presence is very real. But, thankfully, things are changing so that there can be real give-and-take, a genuine exchange between these leaders and those they serve.

The examples of ministry that we have given show that the public side of ministry can provide spiritual nourishment and energy. Spiritual growth and sensitivity can occur along the lines as well as in the angles.

Another avenue to the discernment of the Spirit along the lines of ministry comes through the recognition of gifts. We are not quite sure when and how we receive spiritual gifts. Pentecostals tend to believe the gifts are distributed through the baptism of the Spirit; sacramentarians place the gifts in the waters of baptism; and evangelicals look to conversion as the time when gifts are given. But we tend to think that gifts are given in creation and are awakened by the Spirit — sometimes in baptism, sometimes in conversion, and sometimes in a special filling with or revelation of the Spirit. Perhaps the "when" and "how" of spiritual gifts pale in importance when compared to the "that" — that we have been blessed with gifts, that we recognize them, and that we use them to the glory of God.

Isn't it obvious that when persons have gifts for the ministries to which they have been called, the work is easier and more effective? And isn't it equally obvious that nothing can be more frustrating for people than to serve in situations for which they are not gifted? A spirituality of ministry for the new day in the church must include careful attention to the discernment of gifts and the matching of gifts to calling.

Another opening to the spirituality along the lines comes through sensing the Presence in another person or in a situation. Ministry along the lines often takes place in situations like the ones we've described — situations that involve teaching, preaching, or administering, and pastoral care. The Presence of the Spirit is always there but often acts with such subtlety and gentleness that the untrained eye fails to notice. Yet, in the person who is truly looking, listening, and sensing, the Presence can be named and affirmed.

Take Willie, for example. The Presence in him beamed a confidence and a hope that spoke louder than words. It wasn't possible to go into his room without being aware that he had been anointed to die, and the power of that anointing engulfed all in the room. Even in the midst of sadness and impending loss, the Spirit nurtured the faith and hope of the pastor and all the church members who came for a farewell visit.

The spirituality of the servant of God, whether clergy or lay, is affirmed and enhanced through words spoken to him or her along the lines. Alert disciples of Christ learn to listen for the affirming and directing voice of Christ in the ongoing work of ministry. Some church members often lavish praise on the preacher for a thoughtful sermon or on a fellow member for an act of kindness. Some of these affirmations seem culturally motivated, but the discerning servant of God can distinguish between the polite words of appreciation and the word spoken through Christ.

That word may be heard during a visit with a terminally ill person like Willie. He told his pastor, "So many times in your sermons, your prayers, and your visits, I've felt the presence of God. You have indeed been my minister." That may well have been Christ speaking to the pastor.

And when an elder like Paul Anderson tells his wife, "Tonight I encountered Christ in this administrative session of the church," he indicates an awareness of Christ in the business of the church. Perhaps these words of Christ come by indirection, but they are nevertheless an authentication of his Presence among us.

The spirituality of ministry finds its life not only along the lines in doing the work but also in moments of reflection on the experiences of giving and receiving, listening and discerning, and hearing the words of others as Christ's words. The words spoken in the give-and-take of ministry often etch themselves in the memory of God's servants. And one day, when a weary pastor or a hardworking elder takes a few minutes to relax, he or she sits down and remembers. The memory preserves more than a naked outline of a Habitat house being built or a well-delivered sermon or a Spirit-led elder's meeting; it also holds a recollection of meeting God along the lines of ministry. And when the servants of Christ recall these encounters, amazing things happen in their spiritual lives. They experience a growing capacity to notice God's presence in every part of life. Clarity about their calling increases. Thankfulness grows.

Probably the most important aspect of this active memory is that it assures the servants of Christ that they are not alone in the work of ministry. The God who called them not only goes with them but also goes before them into the struggles of the day. And remembering that healing is taking place in the lives they touch through their ministry brings them hope, and thus offers them a persistent assurance that their ministry is not in vain. Remembering nourishes the soul with images of those days when God made Godself known to people in extraordinary ways in ordinary places. Remembering reminds us how all the marches along the lines of ministry not only make a difference in the Kingdom of God but also give strength and courage to God's agents.

QUESTIONS FOR REFLECTION AND DISCUSSION

1. What is a "spirituality of the lines"?
2. How is a spirituality of the lines different from a "spirituality of the angles"?
3. Which best describes your congregation's spirituality? Your own?
4. What do you need to learn from the other approach?

SUGGESTIONS FOR JOURNALING

1. Complete this sentence with two or three paragraphs: "I feel closer to God when I . . ."
2. Read over what you've written. Are you nurtured most by the lines or by the angles?
3. Complete this sentence: "If I were to explore my spiritual life from the other perspective, I would . . ."
4. Write a brief letter to God expressing the desire that has arisen out of your reflection.

Chapter Three

A SPIRITUALITY
GROUNDED IN THE WORD

While thoughtful and deeply dedicated leaders reject a superficial spirituality, they wisely do not create their own spirituality *de nouveau*. Rather, they turn to the long and rich tradition that reaches back more than twenty-five centuries to discover how God's people have experienced the Divine Presence and have expressed it in the texts of Holy Scripture. These texts have been written, edited, preserved, believed, and lived for over thirty-five hundred years. The substance of these texts, having been oral for generations, reaches far back in human memory: these communications of faith were heard, memorized, and repeated until the time they were committed to writing and canonized as our sacred texts.

In response to their encounter with the holy, the writers of the sacred texts sought to express in words what their eyes had seen, their ears had heard, and their hearts had felt. They could not, however, capture the Absolute either in their narratives or in their descriptive statements. What they did was to give testimony to their visions and ecstasies, their fears and doubts, their musings and longings. Their testimonies pointed their readers toward the Divine and opened a window on God's character and works.

Leaders who are seeking God's Presence in their lives and in the church today will surely appreciate the work done by the historical community of faith that has given us a dependable vision of the presence and activity of the living God. For three millennia men and women of faith have diligently studied these texts, practiced them, and spent countless hours copying and preserving them. We are the recipients of all their labors.

In the Bible, therefore, we have a collection of books that record faithful people's experiences of God's self-revelation and the different responses that the chosen people, the church, and the unbelieving world have made to it. The material in this sacred account of divine action and speech offers the paradigm for an emerging Christian spirituality. A person seeking to know God's will and give leadership to God's people would be foolish to ignore the long experience of those who have followed this way. How nearsighted for persons in our day to label these texts irrelevant if they have never looked at them in depth or sought to encounter God's eternal Presence through them! Yet even among those who have carefully studied these texts there are varying opinions of their meaning and significance. Not all segments of the Christian community agree about these texts and the manner in which they are to be interpreted for today.

Contrasting Approaches to the Text

While the Christian community deeply affirms the sacred nature of the biblical text, challenging questions continue to arise. For instance, what are we to do with the Old Testament stories that describe God's unprovoked violence against nations? How are we to receive New Testament accounts which suggest that women are of less value or have lesser abilities than men? How do we respond to rules and commandments that seem far from our own world, with its virtual realities, quantum physics, cloning techniques, and destruction of God's creation? How can any material written two thousand years ago in the dead languages of cultures now completely foreign to us address the twenty-first-century soul?

In general, responses to such questions in contemporary Western culture have taken three dominant routes, each one a version of rationalism, each one forgetting the mystery of God that lies at the core of the sacred Scriptures. These rationalistic responses suggest two things: (1) that Scripture primarily offers us clear doctrinal truths about God and instruction in how to conform our behavior and understanding to these truths; and (2) that we uncover this information by applying our minds to studying what the text states.

The first rational response to Scripture simply rejects the biblical tradition and all things Christian — or at least all things "churchy." "Surely," say many modern students of the Bible, "we cannot take seriously writings that seem at best obtuse and at worst contradictory to the grace we long to experience. If God is like this [referring to narrowly defined doctrinal truths about God], and we are to be formed in God's image [believe and behave in a narrowly prescribed way], Christianity is destructive of the human spirit rather than life-giving." This attitude does prevail in our culture, presenting us with a mission field much like the one Paul faced in the first century. So, as leaders of God's people, how do we embrace the Word of God in life-giving ways, and how do we help others in the congregation do the same?

A second rational response represents the other side of the coin. This second way encompasses the popular media's dominant portrait of Christianity — and in large part represents what the first response rejects. This response embraces various degrees of literalism. It also assumes that the biblical text first and foremost presents narrowly, accurately, and clearly stated truths about God and a godly life. But where the first response begins by being skeptical about the accuracy of narrow truths, the second proceeds unquestioningly, embracing the literal truth in the text. Thus, when the information presented by the biblical text seems to contradict cultural values, the text is not open to critique or questioning. Instead, this biblical information is blindly grasped and proclaimed.

A third response also seeks information from the biblical text. It arises out of the tradition of Enlightenment scholarship. Unlike the first response, it begins from a position of faith, affirming the sacred nature of the text. Unlike the second response, this third way is more apt to critique the text in light of contemporary culture, rejecting what does not fit. Using the tools of modern research, this approach examines the authorship, authenticity, and veracity of each of the biblical texts. It seeks to explain the framework of the original languages in which the Scriptures were written and the context that shaped them. In addition, it carefully analyzes the various literary forms employed and notes the similarities and differences between our sacred texts and those of other religions. This careful analysis attempts to discover in the Bible broad truths about God and life with God, truths that are big enough to fit shifting cultural sensibilities and historical settings.

Actually, all of these responses can offer church leaders certain benefits in the new century if we do not embrace any one of them in its entirety. The first, a rejection of Scripture, keeps us on our spiritual toes. Can we be so sure we are always right, always on God's side, when most of the people we encounter each day are deeply suspicious of the faith we profess? These brothers and sisters, who are, like us, created in the image of God, echo Micah's reminder that we are required to dwell humbly with God. The second response, that of biblical literalism, points us toward deep trust in God and God's Word, a trust that can hold out against the storms of cultural shifts and trends. It reminds us that we ultimately rest in God, and it is to God that we must look for guidance in our lives. And the third response, the response of critical scholarship, helps us see that we are to keep searching for God's truth. It enhances our understanding while it reminds us that God and divine truth cannot be nailed down or fitted into one theological box because there is always more to learn and more to uncover.

However, in spite of the benefits these approaches to Scripture may offer, each ultimately fails to deeply nourish our lives with God. Those who reject the text, of course, will not receive its richness, its holy beauty, its offer of God's Presence. Those who engage it literally may miss the mystery and grace of a God who is deeper and broader than human beings can imagine. And those who affirm only critical analysis may miss the sense of reverence evidenced by the early writers and the scribal hands of monks who prayed their way through these texts even as they laboriously made copies. They may also miss solid grounding in the eternal Spirit of Love mediated by the Word. In a strange way, each of these approaches to the text seems to model a different way of responding to God. In the first approach, the text is dismissed; in the second, it is made into an idol; and in the third, it is bound by human techniques.

It is all too obvious that Christians who read and study the Bible — whether they tend toward literalism or Enlightenment-inspired critical analysis — can do so without encountering the God of the texts, the Holy Presence that inspired the actions which gave birth to the interpretations and the writing. The Christian who treats the Scriptures this way is like an agronomist who researches, studies, and analyzes the manner in which wheat sprouts and matures but never eats the bread produced from the wheat. When we approach the text looking primarily for information, both scholarship in the academy and in the pastor's study can give us vast knowledge about the husk and kernel of the texts, but no bread, no sustenance. When a person is starving, she is not interested in seed, fertilizer, and grain. She wants and needs bread.

Pastors and lay leaders who have fed themselves on the texts can make bread for the hungry. This bread has many forms, from prayer to preaching, from committee meetings to acts of mercy. But how can these texts, as we say, make bread? First, many of us need to shift our perspective on Scripture, moving from what it is to how it speaks to us. The tendency is to see the Bible as a delivery system of clear information about God. If the Bible primarily delivers clear, specific information, then our task as leaders would be to find the key that will unlock this sacred container, open it, and apply to our lives the information we find there.

Interestingly, this one-dimensional approach to Scripture that seems to dominate the Western church today has not always dominated biblical interpretation. Christians throughout the church's history generally have approached Scripture as a sacred setting for encountering the Presence of God. Gathering information has been but one part of what happens within that sacred setting and, at best, a secondary concern until recent years.

Origen, a third-century theologian, illustrates the meditative approach to Scripture. In the introduction to a volume of his works, editor Rowan A. Greer states, "Origen's piety is Scriptural more than it is sacramental. By meditating on the word of God the Christian begins to contemplate the eternal mysteries that supply the motive, power, and goal of the Christian life." This assessment is illustrated in Origen's meditation on the creation of humankind in the "Commentary on the Song of Songs":

> At the beginning of Moses' words, where he describes the creation of the world, we find reference to two men that were created, the first made after the image and likeness of God and the second formed from the dust of the ground. Paul the Apostle well knew this and possessed a clear understanding of these matters. In his letters he wrote more openly and clearly that every person is two different men. This is what he said, "Though our outer man is wasting away, our inner man is being renewed every day," and further, "For I de-

light in the law of God in my inner man." . . . On this basis I think that no one ought now to doubt that Moses at the beginning of Genesis wrote about the making or forming of two men, when he sees Paul, who understood better than we do what was written by Moses, saying that every person is two different men.[1]

In these words Origen records his meditation on the nature of human beings in both their inward and their outward form. He understands that both sides of our nature affect our relationship with God. When we listen to the text of Scripture, we are renewed by the Spirit of God inwardly, even though our bodies are wasting away. Origen brings himself to the text to expose his life, to encounter God, not merely to find new information about God.

Learning information about God and God's ways will enhance our encounter with God, but the Bible offers us much more than facts. It is this writing that most fully offers us God's intimate Presence — whether in praying Scripture, studying it, hearing it, reading it, singing it, repeating it, memorizing it, acting it out, wrestling with it, fearing it, trusting it, finding comfort in it, or being challenged by it. Embracing Scripture as a setting for meeting God, rather than as a repository of half-hidden information, frees us to explore ever more fully God's Presence with us. We no longer have to find either a special meaning or the one true meaning in every passage.

But this is not to say that certain passages of Scripture don't speak more vividly to people at certain times. During various periods in the life of the Christian church, for example, particular portions of Scripture have been more meaningful than others. The desert fathers and mothers took with great seriousness the text that commanded them to sell all that they had and follow Jesus. Martin Luther was driven by the text proclaiming, "The just shall live by faith," and the first missionaries of the new era heard clearly Jesus' commission, "Go into all the world and preach the gospel." Similarly, each of us at certain points in our lives may find more meaning in some parts of Scripture than in others. And that is as it should be. If we approach Scripture as a setting for meeting God rather than as a box full of information, we can trust that through these texts we will meet

1. *Origen,* ed. Rowan Greer (New York: Paulist Press, 1979), p. 220.

God and that God will begin transforming us, whether or not we receive a particular message, particular information, from the text. God will meet us in new and unexpected ways as we engage the Word.

Even passages that deeply offend us can become places for encountering God. When we are troubled by what we read and the Word repels us, we must examine what is happening within us. Suppose that a committed Christian is deeply offended by an Old Testament passage that describes God destroying all the people of a nation whose king resists the people of Israel. In spite of careful, critical study of the passage, her overwhelming response is to reject the text as simply an outdated characterization of God, a text not revelant to her life. A more fruitful approach would be to follow her study of the text with an exploration of the nature, shape, and direction of her experience of the passage. Questions she might ask herself include these: What is prompting my revulsion? Why am I reacting in this way? What would I prefer to see happen in the story? What longing lies underneath that preference? In what way is that longing a reflection of my desire for God and God's way (or not)? As I move away from the kind of situation described in the text, where am I experiencing God's Presence (or not)?

Such an approach acknowledges the sacred nature of the written Word by affirming the belief that encountering Scripture always places us before God. Even in the midst of repulsion, we can look for how we are attracted to God. Rather than allow our repugnance at a particular portion of Scripture to cause us to reject the text, we can note how it points us to God. Instead of dismissing the text — and the experience of God's Presence that comes with it — we can receive an opportunity to deepen our sensibility for the Divine. By attending to how God is present in our response to Scripture, every text, whether offensive to us or appealing, offers an invitation to explore life with God ever more deeply.

Meeting God in Scripture

In an effort to help you learn to meet God in Scripture, we want to suggest further ways of engaging the text that might lead from the kernel of information to the bread that waits to be eaten. We will concentrate on four ways in which the sacred text brings us into transformative intimacy with God — by speaking a message to us, by slowly nourishing us, by placing us in the story, and by inspiring the imagination.

Scripture and the Metaphors of Life

Consider human life as a metaphor for our dealing with the text. The truth of the text has the power to connect us with the intimate Presence and action of God that dwells in, around, and through the texts, and to usher us into the reality that gave birth to the texts. Through this encounter with the life of the texts, the Holy Spirit can enliven our lives. No one has written with greater clarity or conviction about the important role of the Spirit in enlivening Scripture than John Calvin. He declares that the inner testimony of the Spirit is essential for our appropriation of the texts. The Spirit transforms our lives by speaking through the texts of Scripture, allowing them to speak a message of truth to us.

When we consider the text in relationship with our own experience, a number of life-related metaphors suggest themselves. Take conception, for example. Reflect on the moment when the angel came to Mary, announcing to her that the Holy Spirit would come upon her and that she would conceive "the Word of God" in her womb. What a shocking message that she, a human being, would become pregnant with the revelation of God! The God of Israel would actually take up residence in her body, and she would bear that Presence in all her activities. In a similar way the Spirit overshadows the text and causes it to conceive truth in the mind of the reader. Through this action of the Spirit, the truth of the Word begins to grow in the soul like a fetus in the womb. And faithful Christians carry in themselves this truth-inspired Presence of the Holy.

And this conception can result in transformation and rebirth. Consider this example. In the darkness of a painful experience, a servant of God hears the echo of this text: "But the steadfast love of the Lord endures forever." This word of grace, like a womb, surrounds and nourishes the heart and soul with the assurance of God's Presence. And this person, as he or she becomes more and more filled with a sense of God's Presence, will not — cannot — let the relationship go. Day after day the relationship grows and grows until a new person emerges.

In addition, the resurrection from death to life offers a metaphor for

39

God's coming alive in the heart of the searching person. Think of the text of Scripture as a dead body in a tomb upon which the Spirit breathes. When the Spirit infuses the text with life, it rises from the dark, damp tomb of ignorance or irrelevance and comes alive in the awareness of the reader, speaking directly to her about herself and her relation to God.

A pastor, for example, finds herself struggling with the call to ministry. Her life has come unglued; her old certainties about herself and her role have suddenly been shot through with doubt. She wonders if she can go on as an ordained minister of the gospel. In addition to these self-doubts, her marriage has disintegrated into conflict, and the specter of divorce hangs over her head. Then one morning in her search she reads Romans 11:29 — "The gifts and the calling of God are irrevocable" — and in that moment the Spirit breathes upon that text, and it leaps from the page into her consciousness and pours a healing balm upon her troubled heart. In that fleeting moment, these words from another time and place become the Word of God here and now for a staggering soul looking for support and hope.

God does not forsake those whom God has called. God's faithfulness was true for Israel; it is true for us. God has not had a change of heart about our call or about us.

Jesus' teaching about the vine and the branches draws upon another life metaphor, the life-giving sap in the vine. Jesus said, "I am the true vine, and my Father is the vinegrower. He removes every branch in me that bears no fruit. Every branch that bears fruit he prunes to make it bear more fruit. . . . I am the vine, you are the branches." (See John 15:1-10.) The Word of God joins us to Christ — God's speech, purpose, and power. And when we are joined to Christ, his life flows into us and through us. We are made alive through Christ's life.

This life-giving power in the Vine often flows into us and gives us new assurance that overcomes our doubts. Take the layperson, for instance, who has wondered about her acceptance with God. One day while reading this "vine and branches" passage, these words literally leap from the page: "You did not choose me but I chose you. And I appointed you to go and bear fruit" (John 15:16). In these words of Jesus she receives such a direct answer to her questioning that it seems like a telegram sent immediately to her from her Lord.

Scripture and the Metaphors of Eating and Feeding

Persons who are seeking God's Presence through Scripture without resorting to one of the types of rationalism may draw on a very ancient process called *Lectio Divina*. This approach to Scripture is analogous to eating a fine meal; it is "feeding" on the texts. *Lectio* was first practiced by the hermits in the Egyptian desert while they sat by their cells weaving mats. The method was further developed in the monasteries of the West. As early as the sixth century, Saint Benedict taught his monks this way of "feeding" on the Word of God. This approach to Scripture serves us well in our effort to hear God speak in our day.

The five dimensions of this process of encountering the Word through the words include reading, ruminating, meditating, praying to God, and contemplating the text. Perhaps these movements are obvious or already known to some of you. But for those of you to whom this is new, here is how it might look in practice.

First, you read. You open your Bible to the third chapter of the Epistle of James and read,

> So also the tongue is a small member, yet it boasts of great exploits. How great a forest is set ablaze by a small fire! And the tongue is a fire. The tongue is placed among our members as a world of iniquity; it stains the whole body, sets on fire the cycle of nature, and is itself set on fire by hell. For every species of beast and bird, of reptile and sea creature, can be tamed and has been tamed by the human species, but no one can tame the tongue — a restless evil, full of deadly poison. (James 3:5-8)

When you read this text, a small sentence leaps out at you: "And the tongue is a fire." You then ruminate (the second dimension) on this sentence by repeating it over and over, chewing on it like a cow chews its cud. This ruminating is like chewing two different foods at once, with one food attracting another and mixing with saliva before your swallow it. In this process of ruminating, the original message of the text expands and opens you to other aspects of your life.

Then you meditate on the text (the third dimension). You begin to consider what the notion of "the tongue is a fire" might have to do with your life. You ask of yourself and God, "What does it mean that 'the tongue is a fire'? How is my tongue a fire?" And as you ask God this question, incidents begin coming to your mind. You recall the rude manner in which you spoke to the clerk at the grocery store, and the memory evokes a further prayer for forgiveness. You may consider how to speak the next time and ask for grace, or perhaps you may feel strongly enough about your failure to make an apology to the clerk. You begin to wonder how you can control your tongue. It seems so hard, nearly impossible for you to be in control of this tiny member. Then your mind shifts to Christ — he can control your tongue. Perhaps you think, "If he can control my tongue, then he can control other passions that distance me from God." At this point the meditation can continue in numerous directions, revealing other barriers in your relation to Christ.

Eventually you will want to pray to God (the fourth dimension). Perhaps you will pray quietly within your heart, or perhaps you will speak aloud. You may decide to mold clay to shape a prayer offering to God that symbolizes your confession of a "fiery tongue." Or you may have recalled during your meditation how your tongue spoke words that hurt a co-worker. The wounding was unintentional; nevertheless, your words cut deeply into her heart and brought tears to her eyes. Now you pray that your tongue may be brought under control and disciplined like a mule with a bit between its teeth. And you may think of similar instances when misunderstandings in the church or elsewhere resulted in harsh words that damaged relationships. You express to God your concerns, your fears, and your hopes about these incidents as well.

The fifth dimension in *Lectio Divina* is contemplating. Contemplation is a studied silence in the Presence of God. This is where the text ultimately leads you: to stillness and quiet in the Divine Presence. No longer is your effort involved in prayer. Your effort is stilled. You are contentedly caught up in God's Presence and activity. Your intention-filled meditation has ended, and your self-directed expressions of prayer have ceased. Here in the presence of God the tongue of your mind has also been silenced, and you are reduced to wordlessness.

This time of contemplation is different for everyone. For some, this time is filled with an absence of images and feelings. As this sense of absence increases, the indescribable sense of God's Presence grows. For those from a different tradition within Christianity, this time is filled with images and feelings that come unbidden, without any effort on their part. As these visions and feelings increase in intensity, these individuals experience God's Presence more powerfully. Perhaps in contemplation we experience our proper place before God: all effort is stilled as we are nurtured by communion with the One who made us.

The five dimensions of *Lectio Divina* do not necessarily follow in a systematic, progressive order. For instance, prayers directed to God may flow from contemplation and become words for rumination, meditation, and further contemplation. The ancients likened this process to a cow chewing its cud: we swallow the words and regurgitate them in a new form to be chewed again. And all the while this sacred food nourishes and sustains and forms us into a living word.

Can you imagine what our churches would be like if pastors gathered with searching lay leaders to engage Christ through his Word in this fashion? Don't you think we would lose some of our reticence in speaking about God if we prayed together in depth?

Scripture and Participation in Its Story

We have seen how the text comes alive for us in the metaphors of life (birth, resurrection, sap in the vine) and also through the five movements of *Lectio Divina* — reading, ruminating, meditating, praying, and contemplating. But there is still another way in which the Word speaks powerfully through the words. We can actually enter into the texts and participate in their action. This engagement of the text works well with the narrative portions of Scripture.

To a large extent, the way of participation in texts was identified and developed by Ignatius of Loyola more than five centuries ago. Although this way of engaging narratives in Scripture can also be seen in traditions as ancient as the desert fathers and mothers and the fathers of the Eastern Church, it finds full expression in the writings of Ignatius and the Jesuits. As Ignatius prayed the Bible texts, he noticed that the passages he prayed brought images and sensations to his consciousness. So he began deliberately placing himself in the scenes where Jesus was teaching or healing by using all his senses to participate in the scene. For example, he imagined the weather, the feel of the dirt beneath his feet, the sounds and even the smells of the incident. For him this participation in the events of Jesus' life was "contemplation."

Whereas in *Lectio Divina* the one who is praying often enters into a stillness of awareness, an absence of images and thoughts and feelings, in the Ignatian approach one always seeks a state of active contemplation. Ignatius understands contemplation as being filled with images, sensations, and a profound awareness of Christ. Here is a version of the process that Ignatius describes in his *Spiritual Exercises.*

Read a text like the healing of the leper in Mark 1:40-46:

> A leper came to him begging him, and kneeling he said to him, "If you choose, you can make me clean." Moved with pity, Jesus stretched out his hand and touched him, and said to him, "I do choose. Be made clean!" Immediately the leprosy left him, and he was made clean. After sternly warning him he sent him away at once, saying to him, "See that you say nothing to anyone; but go, show yourself to the priest, and offer for your cleansing what Moses commanded, as a testimony to them." But he went out and began to proclaim it freely, and to spread the word, so that Jesus could no longer go into a town openly, but stayed out in the country; and people came to him from every quarter.

Imagine that you are present at the healing. Think about the day, the weather, the surroundings, the people who are present, the feelings you have, and your expectations. Use your senses of sight, sound, smell, and touch to feel what it would have been like to have been there, observing Jesus heal the leper. Imagine what it was like for the leper. Imagine what it was like for the disciples who were standing by.

Think of yourself as the leper. In what ways are you the leper? What does it feel like to be a leper? Pray the prayer he offered to Jesus: "If you choose, you can make me clean." Listen to Jesus' response: "I do choose. Be made clean!"

Imagine that everyone else has left the scene. Only you and Jesus remain. During this encounter, what questions come to your mind? What do you wish to ask Jesus? Ask him. Wait for an answer. Then write down what you hear him saying. Read over the inspirations and seek discernment about whether this was indeed Christ speaking or your own imagination working or a combination of both.

Participating in the text in this manner can give you enormous spiritual energy and a sense of the immediate Presence of Christ. You can find yourself in the narratives of Jesus' healing and teaching, and by participating in them you will feel yourself drawn closer to God.

This approach to Scripture offers the leaders of Christ's church a kind of nurture that will both heal and transform their leadership. The nurturing power, however, comes not in a message received. Instead, it comes through experiencing an image — that is, with every dimension of their being: mind, emotions, senses, body, imagination. For many people, this image and the deep feeling that goes with it linger in their lives for years. This experience of God's Presence also becomes a spiritual touchstone, something to which they can return time and again in prayer. Here is one man's description of such an experience:

> Some years ago I was praying the Easter story, imagining myself with the women in the garden. We came to the empty tomb, and then only Jesus and I were there. He was a young man in white clothing. As Jesus approached me, I began to feel nervous. I'd never had an experience of Jesus before — just a sense of God, God as powerful light or warmth surrounding me. So this was completely new for me. What would happen? What would he say? What should I say? And then a strange thing happened. Jesus stretched out his arms, took my hands, and slowly began to lead me in a dance. In a few moments two other persons — a wise elderly figure and a young woman in colorful, flowing robes — joined us. It was incredible — a slowly moving circle dance with the Trinity; I began to feel light and free. My looming fears and anxieties were melting away. We danced and danced in the garden, a resurrection dance. Since that time, my prayers are often full of that garden dance. I can return there in an instant for a taste of God's love and a sense of healing.

For this man, the image that came to him in prayer became a dominant metaphor for his life with God. In times of need, celebration, discernment, fear, and longing, the image of dancing with God guided, inspired, and sustained him.

Scripture and Imaginative Hermeneutics

An essential way of dealing with Scripture requires us to interpret ancient texts for modern times. In other words, we must leap from the first century to the twenty-first century through an imaginative interpretation. Whether minister or laity, we all finally interpret the text. Text-grounded leaders interpret the text not only for themselves but also for the congregation. The one question that always confronts us as leaders is, How do we get from the past to the present? How do we take the questions of today and find help in these ancient texts?

The task of interpretation is a daring imaginative enterprise. Remember those two words: "daring" and "imaginative"! This risky act in which we leap from the first century to the twenty-first requires being grounded in the truth of the text for that time and place and imaginatively applying its truth to issues with which we struggle today.

You might take the experience of Peter in the tenth chapter of Acts as an illustration of the work of a daring imagination. Recall the experience of Peter:

> About noon the next day, as they were on their journey and approaching the city, Peter went up on the roof to pray. He became hungry and wanted something to eat; and while it was being prepared, he fell into a trance. He saw the heaven opened and something like a large sheet coming down, being lowered to the ground by its four corners. In it were all kinds of four-footed creatures and reptiles and birds of the air. Then he heard a voice saying, "Get up, Peter; kill and eat." But Peter said, "By no means, Lord; for I have never eaten anything that is profane or unclean." The voice said to him again, a second time, "What God has made clean, you must not call profane." This happened three times, and the thing was suddenly taken up to heaven. Now while Peter was greatly puzzled about what to make of the vision that he had seen, suddenly the men sent by Cornelius appeared. They were asking for Simon's house and were standing by the gate. (Acts 10:9-17)

The issue for Peter was the distinction between the "clean" and the "unclean" and how he should relate to the unclean. In his vision on the

46

roof, Peter was told to get up and kill and eat four-footed creatures, reptiles, and birds of the air — food unclean for a Jew. Peter refused because his culture had instilled in him that he must never touch — much less eat — these unclean animals. He had been taught that eating these animals was an abomination. And up to this point in his life he had never done so. But the Voice said, "What God has made clean, you must not call profane." Three times the message came to him. As the vision faded, men from the house of Cornelius (the Roman centurion who had been instructed by God to send for Peter) stood knocking at the door. As it turned out, the vision was not so much about eating unclean animals as it was about going to the house of a Gentile, since Gentiles were also considered unclean by the Jews.

What can we extrapolate from this text today? Let's take the issue of homosexuals in the church. In earlier times, they were suspected, vilified, and often shunned. But today, with the increasing evidence that people are born with different sexual orientations, and the understanding that we are all God's children, these attitudes are changing.

This is but one illustration of an imaginative interpretation of the text. And, we should point out, every interpretation of the text is imaginative, for the Word travels from there to here on the wind of imagination.

If we take Peter's experience as a paradigm, we see that what God spoke to the Israelites in the past was changed with Peter's vision. Can you imagine how difficult it must have been for Peter to listen to the Spirit that told him to act contrary to the ways he had been taught all his life? Peter surely must have received enormous courage from the vision that empowered him to go to Cornelius's house. Isn't it strange that had he not had this courage — and had the community of faith not had the courage to listen to the Spirit of God — perhaps the Gentiles would not have been included in the church, and the Gospel would have faded as the message of a Jewish sect?

We hope these four ways of engaging the text will enrich and enliven your spirituality, and draw you ever closer to the Divine Presence.

47

QUESTIONS FOR REFLECTION AND DISCUSSION

1. Which of the three rational ways of dealing with texts have you most of-ten resorted to?
2. How do you think listening for God in the texts would change your prac-tice of reading Scripture?
3. Can you relate an incident in your life when you found the text to be a metaphor of life or of eating and feeding? Do you recall an imaginative interpretation of a text that was important to you?

SUGGESTIONS FOR JOURNALING

1. Read the story of the leper in Mark 1.
2. Write a personal account of the incident as if you were standing there ob-serving the encounter. Be sure to tell the story in the first person and describe how your senses were affected by being present that day.
3. Imagine that the leper and the disciples have left the scene, leaving you alone with Jesus. Kneel before him and write down what you wish him to do for you. Record his response. Continue the dialogue until you have five or six interchanges.

Chapter Four

MYTH IN CONGREGATIONAL
SPIRITUALITY

A myth lives in every congregation, an invisible force that imposes it-self on the worship service, influences the official meetings, and hovers over the whole congregation. This invisible power had its birth at the first gathering of the church and has been growing ever since. It has drawn its life from the decisions that were made at the organizing meetings, from the dominant voices of leaders through the years, and from the potent imagination of various members. Sometimes the minister has tried to harness this power and at other times has simply been its victim. The name we give to this invisible force is myth, the church's story.

Every church has a myth and lives and ministers in the power of it. The congregation interprets events in its life through this myth, this narrative it has constructed, and makes strategic decisions according to the values of this mythic account of its corporate life.

Claiming so much power for the myth may sound strange to those leaders who do not know about its formation and role in congregational life. They may even define *myth* so that it seems irrelevant. For example, if they think that myth belongs in the category of fairy tales and believe that such stories have no place in the modern world, they will likely ignore the presence of this invisible force that affects every act of ministry. Yet, the church's myth may constitute one of the most commanding elements in shaping the ministry of a congregation. Either the myth of your congregation supports and empowers the spiritual life of the community, or it resists and confuses it.

The myth may cause the church to reject strangers, or it may support a vote to stop a ministry to the poor. It often determines whether a church retains its present location or moves to a new one. The values and practices buried in the myth can get pastors into serious difficulty, and, when they are not recognized and dealt with, they can unconsciously influence congregational decisions. Yet the myth can also become a powerful ally in the church's ministry and outreach.

What is this invisible, mythic force that so powerfully shapes a congregation's life and ministry? How can it be recognized and dealt with in a creative, constructive manner so that it gives birth to innovative expressions of the kingdom, rather than maintaining the status quo? In brief, how can a church's myth nurture the spiritual life of the whole community and empower it for the mission of Christ?

Defining a Church's Myth

A church's myth is a narrative created by a congregation through its interpretation of the things that have happened to it. It is the story, based on its perception and interpretive imagination, out of which a particular church lives and ministers. The particular lenses of faith worn by the congregation and its leaders also influence the shape and power of the myth. The very nature of myth causes it to embody the holy, because the congregation believes that God has been involved in the events of its life and in the interpretation it has given to those events. For this reason the myth of a congregation takes on a sacred character and often becomes untouchable.

The myth generally begins with the founding members. At the first gathering they have no history together, no tradition, and thus no myth, except the fragments imported from previous congregations. But as soon as the founding group begins to take shape, they share dreams and hopes, fears and needs, and a community begins to be born. At this stage, the "I" of a hundred individuals becomes a "we" — a community that will share its life now and into the future. The things that occur in the life of a church when it is new and as it grows are too numerous and varied to identify, but with a little imagination you can begin to create the list — the choice of location, the selection of a pastor, the struggles to form a community, the power of certain influential laypersons, the development of crises, and so on. Because of the nature of congregational life, the myth begins at the inception of the church and grows through the years. When the myth remains alive and vital, the congregation edits it, enlarges it, and adds new stories, moving toward a fulfilling conclusion informed by the increasing power of its vision.

The myth gives the church its sense of identity. For example, a church may find itself in a changing neighborhood. Other congregations in the area may choose to move to the suburbs and build new churches, but this one congregation stays. Its myth calls for heroic service and compels it to remain where it is and serve those less fortunate. Staying and serving means risking its own life, but it stays nonetheless. The myth that created its identity also gave it the power to stay and risk its life.

The myth provides the glue that holds the congregation together. Once the myth is in place, many who enter the community through the years either consciously or unconsciously are drawn into it, because it tells them who they are in relation to other church members. As long as the myth is alive and not challenged, it holds the members of the community together.

While a vital myth can serve a church well, an unexamined myth may blind a church to the reality of its situation — to the increasing age of its members, to its dwindling funds, and to its inability to fulfill its original vision. The unexamined myth keeps a church bound to its old vision even when it is no longer appropriate for those particular people of God. When the old myth no longer informs and empowers the church in a new situation, it is broken. The breaking of the myth calls the congregation to open itself to a new vision and thus a new story. But it is extremely difficult for a congregation to question its foundational myth and open itself to a new vision and, thus, a transformation of its myth. In some ways the myth of the congregation takes on the same character as the rational approach to Scripture, which cannot be questioned.

Year after year the ethos of the congregation intertwines itself with the myth. Soon the myth influences the language, norms, values, style, and practices of the congregation. Through this constant interaction between the myth and the life of a people, the myth dominates congregational life very subtly but very effectively.

If you have either pastored or belonged to many congregations, surely

51

this description of the role and power of myth makes sense to you. Perhaps you have studied the subject of congregations and the power of their stories. But too few pastors and lay leaders have taken this factor into account with respect to the spirituality of the congregation or the spirituality of their leadership.

Congregational myth informed the earliest congregations just as it does ours today. Try to imagine the myth of the Corinthian congregation. Paul had come to them, preached the gospel, and formed a small group of baptized believers. The Spirit seemed to fill them and minister through them in startling ways. But out of a confused myth they began to argue about who baptized them and what it meant, especially if they had been baptized by Paul.

So the Apostle Paul wrote to them, seeking to correct the baptismal myth:

> God is faithful; by him you were called into the fellowship of his Son, Jesus Christ our Lord. Now I appeal to you, brothers and sisters, by the name of our Lord Jesus Christ, that all of you be in agreement and that there be no divisions among you, but that you be united in the same mind and the same purpose. For it has been reported to me by Chloe's people that there are quarrels among you, my brothers and sisters. What I mean is that each of you says, "I belong to Paul," or "I belong to Apollos," or "I belong to Cephas," or "I belong to Christ." Has Christ been divided? Was Paul crucified for you? Or were you baptized in the name of Paul? I thank God that I baptized none of you except Crispus and Gaius, so that no one can say that you were baptized in my name. (I did baptize also the household of Stephanas; beyond that, I do not know whether I baptized anyone else.) For Christ did not send me to baptize but to proclaim the gospel, and not with eloquent wisdom, so that the cross of Christ might not be emptied of its power. (1 Cor. 1:9-17)

Do you see how the Apostle seeks to correct parts of the myth that controls the church at Corinth? He sets the story straight and interprets the role of the baptized.

When Paul visited Galatia, he also preached the gospel, baptized believers, equipped leaders for the congregations, and continued on his journey. He focused on Christ and Christ alone for salvation. He emphasized that Christ died for them, Christ arose for them, and Christ lives for them. Through faith they received Christ and all his benefits.

After Paul's departure, however, religious leaders from Jerusalem came into the communities of Galatia. They affirmed the importance of Christ, but they also urged the people to keep the whole law, especially the ritual act of circumcision. This additional storytelling contradicted the original master story that Paul had proclaimed. Their interpretation of the gospel, the mythic view out of which they lived and ministered, had been tampered with in a manner that would destroy the gospel and the community. So significant was this attack on the church that Paul refuted it in no uncertain terms:

> Grace to you and peace from God our Father and the Lord Jesus Christ, who gave himself for our sins to set us free from the present evil age, according to the will of our God and Father, to whom be the glory forever and ever. Amen.

> I am astonished that you are so quickly deserting the one who called you in the grace of Christ and are turning to a different gospel — not that there is another gospel, but there are some who are confusing you and want to pervert the gospel of Christ. But even if we or an angel from heaven should proclaim to you a gospel contrary to what we proclaimed to you, let that one be accursed! As we have said before, so now I repeat, if anyone proclaims to you a gospel contrary to what you received, let that one be accursed! (Gal. 1:3-9)

Paul did not intend to stand by and watch the original story of grace be sacrificed for a mixture of faith and law. His zeal to protect the founding myth was so strong that he even wished those subverting it to be accursed.

A further example can be drawn from a contemporary setting. A minister received a call to a suburban congregation that had had two previous pastors in its thirty-year history. The founding pastor did an acceptable job for the first five years, and then the congregation grew beyond his gifts and capacities. His strength was in visiting the members and caring for them during times of illness, pain, and disillusionment. When he reached the limits of his abilities to organize and administer the church's affairs, he departed, though not without considerable struggle and loss of members. The original myth of this church was "We are a family church that shows abundant care for each member."

The second minister led the congregation for more than twenty years. He preached with style, brought in new members, and built a large educational plant and a new sanctuary. He possessed multiple gifts and used them vigorously to increase congregation size, raise money, and develop a reputation in the larger community. During the last decade of his tenure, he focused his ministry on the grace of God. In his sermons and conversations with congregants he repeatedly emphasized that God loves persons unconditionally and that one needs to do nothing but receive the grace of God. He began connecting everything in life to grace: We worship by grace, serve by grace, give by grace, and live fully by the grace of God.

In a sense he was right about grace, but it is possible that he used the emphasis to cover some of his own failings rather than to provide a pure presentation of the gospel. Because he emphasized grace so much, he seemed to put little emphasis on accountability and responsibility. In particular, he was failing to be accountable and responsible in ways that deeply mattered to the congregation: visitation and pastoral care. This did not sit well with a number of church members, and he eventually departed under a cloud of anger and suspicion. The original myth remained, but it was now wrapped in and permeated by grace.

Then the new minister arrived. Early on in his tenure he heard about the weaknesses of the first minister, and the confusion and frustration created by the second, as well as the congregation's appreciation for his years of strong leadership. But the new pastor did not take the time to hear the story and learn about the myth that directed the life of this congregation. If he had, he would have discovered that his dream to minister from a strong spiritual base would conflict with the dominant myth of a family church now wrapped in grace. Listening to the story also would have revealed that his predecessor had an aversion to the word "spiritual," and he probably would have reshaped the presentation of his spiritual vision.

Further, by asking various members about the original story and dreams of the congregation, he would have learned that they expected a minister to know them and visit them in their homes, especially when they were ill. Whether or not he intended to minister in this fashion, he

54

would have discovered the expectations lying deep in the congregational psyche.

As these examples show, simple stories take on immense importance when we consider them as bearers of the myth. After the initial story establishes the myth, it grows with continuing stories that are perceived through the filters of the myth. We have already suggested how the church's myth shapes its spirituality, but now we will focus more specifically on this relationship.

The Spirituality of the Congregation and Its Myth

From antiquity, the myth has been related to the sacred. Some of the great ancient myths recount the interaction of the gods and their relation to human beings. We do not lose that long association of the myth with the sacred even in a post-modern age because the church's myth still seeks to express in a story what God is doing in and with a particular congregation. Communal spirituality concerns itself with the God-human relationship — how it begins, grows, and expresses itself in a particular group of people. Every congregational myth embodies a worldview that presupposes how God relates to persons in the church and to those in the world.

Joining the church, which in the institutional church implies becoming a child of God, requires answering a list of faith statements. Generally the myth legitimates the practices of the congregation, suggests the forms of acceptable ministry, and determines how the community will be spiritual.

Discovering the Myth

A congregation may be shaped by one or more of a variety of myths, too many to enumerate in a brief chapter, but there are several dominant myths that can be easily identified and used to illustrate the power of myth to shape the spirituality of a church. The country-club myth, for example, marks a church's sense of itself as a "party church." It does not intend to become serious about the demands of Jesus Christ, and yet out of its abundant resources, it will share modestly with the poor. In all likelihood this congregation will expect the minister to serve as its chaplain and to preach sermons that confirm its self-indulgent lifestyle.

A different myth may beget the cultural church. This myth creates a congregation that is deeply grounded in the American way of life, family values, and programs that minister to the congregants' needs. The liturgy of worship, its emphasis underscored by the Christian flag and the American flag standing side by side near the podium, consistently reinforces the congregation's conviction that Christianity is compatible with the values, lifestyle, and goals of the secular culture. Those inside the church seem very much like their neighbors who never enter a church building.

The church of sacrificial service would be created by yet another myth, one that draws its inspiration from the cross of Jesus. The strong influence that shapes this congregation's worship, study, and mission life calls for self-giving through a ministry to the poor and marginalized. Generally speaking, congregations that choose to stay in urban areas fit into this category. Members of these congregations give sacrificially, serve beyond the call of duty, and become deeply involved with those less fortunate than themselves.

Finally, a biblical metaphor, "the body of Christ," may call forth still a different form of congregational life. This congregation envisions the presence of Christ in each of its members, and in their fellowship they become the visible, tangible expression of Christ in the world. The leadership seeks in all decisions to discern the mind of Christ and his will for the community. Once the mission of the congregation has been agreed upon, members are invited to discern their call and employ their gifts to accomplish it. Obviously, this type of congregation will emphasize prayer as the ground of its discernment and its empowerment for ministry.

Even these few examples show the enormous power that myth has in shaping a congregation's life and vision. The myth creates an environment that either supports a biblical spirituality in the community of faith or militates against it. And every church's myth has implications for its leaders. In the country-club church, a minister's suggesting that the elders discern God's call for their mission would likely leave them dumbfounded. Inviting members of the cultural church to question international policy would be asking them to engage issues that they believe fall outside the bounds of religious concern. Calling the service-minded congregation to pray would not be a rarity, but many would rather be active than contemplative in prayer. The "body of Christ" congregation, when planning for its future, would prefer to use traditional Christian discernment processes rather than decision-masking approaches drawn from business management techniques.

Clearly, these varying myths mean that what one church is comfortable with may disquiet another. If a leader is to be effective in developing a spiritual congregation, he or she must first learn about the myth that has given shape to that particular church. The minister cannot affirm a myth without knowing what it is. And no attempts can be effectively made to transform a myth until the congregation is sure that the minister and the leaders understand and appreciate the myth. The minister who enters a new church and begins making changes without first getting the story straight will certainly encounter opposition and will likely destroy credibility at the outset. So how do a minister and the key lay leaders discover, embrace, and engage the myth in a particular congregation?

Leaders can begin to discover the church's myth by listening to its bearers and the specific incarnations of it in their experience. Like researchers, leaders must seek out members who have been in the church for a long period of time and ask them to tell their stories of the church. Answers to the following questions will provide the kinds of information needed to discern the myth:

- Why did this church begin? How do you see the hand of God in its beginning?
- What are the significant experiences you have had together as a congregation?
- Who has provided significant leadership in this congregation? What did they give? What were they like?
- Who were the memorable ministers, and what did they do?
- What ministry of this church are you most proud of?
- How have you experienced God through your participation in this congregation?
- What painful or disappointing things have happened to you as a congregation?
- How does this church help people draw close to God?
- When was the church at its peak? What has been its lowest point?

- What major crisis have you dealt with?
- What do you think God wishes for this congregation?
- What gives you hope for the church's future?

By listening carefully to the stories that emerge in response to these questions, leaders can create a time line of significant events and thus begin to construct the congregation's myth. It is important to talk with a large number of congregants to fill in the blanks of the story.

Leaders are of course interested in the spirituality of their congregation, and so will inquire about and give particular attention to the image of God contained in the myth: What is God like for this congregation? How do they see God working in the world? In what ways has God worked in them? In what ways do they expect God to work through them?

Leaders will also want to consider rather carefully how the members perceive their relationship with God. Does God relate to them in a personal manner? Do they have much experience with prayer? Do they see the Bible primarily as a book that gives them information or as a source that opens them to an experience of God?

Embracing the Myth

Not only is it important for leaders to know the stories, the substance of the myth, but they must also embrace the myth — even when the myth may not seem immediately attractive. The mere fact that leaders inquire about the sacred story of a congregation indicates its importance. As leaders respond to the storytellers and the minister incorporates parts of their story into sermons, the congregation will be reassured that the story is known and appreciated. New leaders should recognize that nothing will connect them more strongly to a congregation than knowing, honoring, and appreciating its story.

We believe that spiritual leaders take another step forward when they begin to speak of the myth as "our" story. When they ask questions about events in the life of the congregation and respond favorably to the actions it has taken in the past, members realize that these leaders have embraced their story. Perhaps this is the most accessible point of entry for leaders who wish to give effective leadership in a congregation.

When leaders schedule times of remembrance and asks members to tell parts of the story, this act announces to the congregation that they value the myth and thus value them. Leaders will find it both simple and rewarding to lead the congregation into a time of recalling and constructing their story. On the appointed evening, members meet in the fellowship hall and gather at tables according to the number of years they have been members of the congregation, from the oldest to the newest members. Each person is asked to list on a piece of poster board the significant things that have happened in the church since he or she joined. When the lists have been completed, each group completes the sentence that begins, "Our church is ...." One by one, each group reads aloud to the whole assembly their list and single-sentence summary. Then the lists are placed around the walls of the fellowship hall. The evening not only provides many interesting insights into the unfolding myth of the church; it also offers validation for those who have been at the heart of its construction.

Following the presentation, the facilitator often asks the groups to gather again to reflect on two questions: (1) What do these experiences tell us about our understanding of God in the life of our church? and (2) What are our personal experiences of God's action in our midst? These questions are aimed at uncovering the spiritual dimension of the story. From the responses the leader will gather impressions about members' worldview and the clarity of their experiences of God.

An experience like this one is valuable in two ways. Not only does it inform the minister about the various perceptions of the myth held by the members, but every member benefits from hearing various versions of the story. Consider how important it is for those who have been in the church for forty years to hear what new members experience in the church and desire from it. An integrative, reflective experience like this one clarifies the concrete manifestations of the myth and also helps develop consensus.

Transforming the Myth

It is possible to transform the myth of a congregation, but "handle with care" is the watchword. A congregation's myth defines its worldview and very soon takes on sacred dimensions. When leaders attempt to alter the membership's view of reality, they must be very cautious. Even the slightest challenge to a person's worldview can be extremely threatening, so wise leaders will be gentle and provide plenty of support when embarking on this task.

In working with the congregation's myth, it is important for leaders to recognize that they cannot challenge it at all without first knowing it and honoring it. Why would anyone wish to dishonor a congregation's view of God? It is important not to be confrontational or to suggest that their perceptions of God are wrong.

When, through his or her discernment, the pastor recognizes that changes must occur in the myth, he or she might begin by calling attention to changes that have occurred in the neighborhood or culture around the congregation or in the church itself. For instance, the church that has been informed by the country-club myth can no longer meet the needs of the present generation that is seeking a very different kind of relationship with God. The minister may point out that persons born after 1975 have a profound interest in knowing God but very little interest in the church as an institution. Likewise, if the more socially relevant church of the 1960s expects to respond to current needs, it must consider changing the angle from which it views the world.

As a strategy, confrontation seldom helps in the effort to change. The pastor might consider inviting members to imagine their life together and their mission in a different way. It might be productive to offer classes on prayer as a way to experience God in new ways. Or to invite the young people on retreats that are real retreats and not mere getaways. Or to share in serving at a homeless shelter and reflect on how those who participated met God in the needs of others. These kinds of experiences can offer participants a safe way to imagine the possibilities for change — to engage in a mental experiment, if you will.

Perhaps this mental experiment could later take form as a genuine experiment. The minister could offer to lead a retreat to help persons explore the spiritual dimensions of life. After the retreat the participants could be invited to evaluate their experience and report to the officials of the church.

This kind of exploration might even extend to a leaders' meeting — say, the pastor and the group of elders. The opening challenge could be to sit together for half an hour in silence before the meeting begins. A passage of Scripture could be chosen for this period of silent reflection. After spending this time in silence before God, no doubt the leaders would conduct the business of the meeting in noticeably different ways.

Most congregations will be willing to engage in contemplative silence as an experiment. Calling the new venture an experiment tells the congregation that if it doesn't work, they can always go back to the safety of the old way.

Some attempts at helping a congregation to become more spiritually sensitive and to grow in their awareness of God will be more successful than others. Leaders need to have the courage to admit that, while some efforts succeed, others fail. They also need to recognize that certain experiments in transformation will have greater meaning to one group than they do to another. The results should be reported to the whole congregation so that it has a sense of ownership in the process.

The Mythmaker Role

The most significant person in the congregation with respect to both maintaining and altering the myth is the minister of the church. For the most part, members of the church would be dumbfounded if they were asked, "What is the myth informing the life of this congregation?" Most members do not live in the abstractions required to answer this question. Their life in the church consists primarily in the concrete stories of their experiences.

But when the minister is aware of the myth, it is different. Such a minister knows that the myth wields great power in relationships and decisions. So the minister must be intentional in both affirming it and challenging it. Consider our suggestion to offer a retreat for young adults in a "country club" congregation. For the sake of illustration, assume that most of the participants had a very positive experience — that many spoke of encountering Christ or meeting God in a new way.

But the minister also needs to realize that these experiences may have minimal influence on the myth unless they are interpreted for the congregation. So, after assessing the retreat, the minister might include a line in his or her sermon like, "There was a time when we were labeled a 'country club church' with a limited religious vision, but things have begun to happen here at the Happy Hill Church. Many of the young adults reported that they met God in a significant way during the weekend away." The minister might also add that new doors of ministry seem to be opening for the congregation. The responsible task force could also report the results of the retreat to the church officers at a monthly gathering. These formal, intentional acts will naturally be supplemented with reports from the individuals who made the retreat.

Each of these initiatives has a way of engaging the old myth and changing it slightly. As these dynamic experiences multiply in the congregation, the myth gradually absorbs the influences and changes accordingly. But leaders need to remember that the process of change is slow and requires patience and persistence.

This kind of change involves genuine transformation of the myth. When new initiatives have been tested, narrated, and attached to the myth, it is transformed into something new. By blending the old and the new, the pastor has engaged in a type of redemptive transformation that offers freedom and openness to the congregation.

For the minister to be effective in this role of transforming the existing myth, he or she must have tremendous support from a group of strong laypersons. No minister should be allowed to undertake such a challenging mission without the support and encouragement of those who share in leadership.

We hope that you see the critical importance of myth as you give spiritual leadership to your congregation.

QUESTIONS FOR REFLECTION AND DISCUSSION

1. What is the meaning of myth? How is it created?
2. What are the seminal aspects of your congregation's myth?
3. How does it energize spiritual life? How does it inhibit it?
4. In what ways does your congregation's myth need to be challenged?

SUGGESTIONS FOR JOURNALING

1. Sketch an outline of the congregation's myth by naming the major turning points in its life. What is the myth woven around these turning points?
2. Imagine that the myth has the capacity to speak. Write a dialogue with the myth, asking it how it inhibits and enhances your spiritual life.

Chapter Five

THE SPIRITUALITY OF VISION

Perhaps nothing paralyzes ministry more than attending committee meetings and preaching week after week without a vision for the church and its ministry. A visionless ministry falls into the fated trap of repeating the same programs and practices with ever-decreasing effect. This blind approach spawns a maintenance ministry focused on the past without innovation for the future. Such a ministry lacks both perspective and daring, and is therefore destined for mediocrity.

Today's leaders cannot afford to give a routine, task-oriented performance in their call as servants of the church. Where there is no vision, the people suffer, and so do their leaders. The kind of vision we are talking about here is a vision of God's call to the church. Vision is the capacity to see clearly — to see the unfolding story of the past, to see the needs and opportunities in the present, and to see images of the invisible future. Where the future is concerned, one needs the gift of hunches about the unmarked path into it.

Vision is the capacity to see the invisible. An oxymoron! A contradiction? How can we see the invisible? Vision is not so much the capacity to document events that lie before us as it is the power to imaginatively project new images upon the screen of the future. A vision that hints of the future does not originate in wishful thinking but draws its energy from an encounter with the One in whom the future exists. If this description of vision seems too abstract, consider what it looks like in the practice of ministry.

A minister serves a small, rural church that for years has attracted farmers, landowners, and teachers. Eventually, as the membership shrinks, he realizes that there are increasingly fewer of these types of persons in the area the church serves. If he is a pastor with vision, he has the capacity to see the doors of this church open to the farm workers, the poor in the community, and the Cambodians who in the last decade have moved into the area. Vision is the capacity to see this congregation with a different face, a diversity of cultures, and eventually a different myth.

Consider the retired naval officer who has become a member of a declining inner-city church. He assesses the state of the church and determines to shoulder responsibility for renewal and redevelopment. At his own expense he visits every inner-city congregation that is doing a commendable ministry in the western United States. He recognizes that some churches are finding answers to cultural changes. Prayerfully he undertakes the task of raising the consciousness of the membership of his own church, and he works closely and prayerfully with the minister to imagine a different future for this church. Vision means that this layman can see this congregation changing its character, transforming its worship, and offering ministries it never before considered.

And consider the suburban church that has a strong membership but that has ceased to grow over the past few years. With the area still developing, people are moving into new neighborhoods surrounding the church, but the church remains static in growth and in spirit. For seventeen years the pastor and the lay leadership have led the worshipping community; now they struggle with how to move into a new future created by demographic changes. Vision draws the minister and the appointed leaders to picture and present an alternative future. Perhaps it will involve a new family-life center, a sports program, a preschool, or a ministry in spiritual formation.

Such vision has radical implications for the focus and work of both pastor and people. Vision focuses on what can be, not on what already exists. Regrettably, it seems to us that not enough leaders in today's churches have this kind of vision. Granted, there are imaginative, future-oriented leaders in every denomination, but their numbers are slim. And without visionary men and women of God, congregations and denominations slip into the repetition of safe practices, which permit members to retain their comfort levels and avoid the risks of growth. Clergy, too, can slip into a comfortable spirituality. Unfortunately, the lay leaders of the church can also come to love their comfort and fail to challenge the minister to more aggressive leadership.

It is imperative that this situation change, because vision is vital to the heart and soul of the church. Vision rests on the shoulders of the church's leaders. No vision can come to fulfillment without the joint effort of both pastor and lay leaders. The pastor brings to the table a sensitivity to the faith of the church and its demands; the lay leaders bring to the table the strategies and costs of moving forward. But neither clergy nor laity can by their own experience and gifts create the vision. The vision we are speaking of comes as a gift from God. We do not mean to depreciate either the minister's training or the lay leaders' experience but to emphasize that the receiving of a vision is a spiritual event involving both the leadership and the whole community. Perhaps both clergy and lay leaders will need to wipe the film from the eyes of their hearts so that they may see more clearly.

Ministry and Vision

Both the spirituality of ministry and the spirituality of the leaders depend on vision. As you probably noticed, we have not given a specific, thorough definition of vision; to do so would squeeze the life out of it. Besides, vision does not yield to measurement. It is not defined or bounded by "vision statements." Yet when we talk with church leaders for even a few minutes, it seems possible to discern whether they are merely doing a job or truly leading in the power of a vision.

All the dominant threads of a healthy spirituality are woven into the fabric of a vision. A vision emerges from an encounter with the Sacred, an encounter with God. Vision, as we understand it, contrasts with brainstorming, weighing the pros and cons of a decision, and deciding on a life plan through an analysis of gifts and possibilities. Thus, a vision is not a final conclusion that is arrived at through a rational process.

Vision, by contrast, comes as a gift; it seems to arise in Another or in the soul's brush with the Other. When vision comes as a gift from the Beyond, it grasps the spirit in a convincing and compelling manner. It fuses with the spirit, but it also engages the mind and the will. The experience both transforms the recipient's way of "seeing" and empowers him or her for engagement.

At various junctures most leaders have been possessed with a vision or have felt the need for one. But the way of the vision can be challenging. How many young pastors have entered the ministry with a burning vision, only to discover overwhelming resistance to the dream they believed God put in their heart? After a year or two, those thin visions have been swept up by the congregational vacuum, never to be released again. And how many elders have been nominated, examined, and ordained by a congregation, only to find strong resistance to their dreams? Too often young visionaries become so discouraged that they cannot wait for their term of service to expire.

In other instances, truly spiritual leaders who in the past faithfully sought a vision with a congregation find that the vision has now been realized. At this point both the leadership and the congregation must seek a new vision or settle for mediocrity.

In other situations, worthy, compelling visions falter when unpredictable occurrences make their fulfillment impossible. In one instance it is a divorce; in another, an accident; in yet another, an illness or the loss of a spouse. Perhaps the community changes, and the old vision no longer fits. In this situation the original vision has been broken, and another must be sought.

We feel quite certain that the vision for the church must be fully shared by the minister because without his or her leadership it can never come to fruition. We also feel that it is important to realize that visions are powerfully affected by where ministers are in their life cycles. One minister at the age of forty seeks a vision for her life because she strongly desires authenticity in herself and her ministry during her most productive years. Another minister at age fifty-five goes to the desert to seek a vision for the final years of his ministry; the remaining years feel too important to trivialize. A minister facing retirement finds the issue of vision surfacing again because she cannot live without purpose. Retirement will not end her life with God or her service in the kingdom of God, but it will change them. Realizing that these final years may be more challenging than all the foregoing ones, the minister seeks a vision for her life beyond the hustle and bustle of active ministry.

These snapshots of a minister at the height, midpoint, and end of active ministry do not take into account certain challenging factors. In the early days of ministry, many young ministers have a great desire to succeed. For them success is measured in terms of money, church membership, and popularity. These forces have the strength to blur God's vision for them and the congregation. They need to work hard to heed the call of the vision. After twenty years of ministry, ministers need to evaluate their vision and values. Have they committed themselves to be God's leaders, or have they settled for something less? At about ten years before retirement, some ministers settle into a comfortable rut. Having had a "successful" ministry, they do not have the courage to dream new dreams and take risks that could undermine their apparent success. At this juncture, pastors desperately need sensitive and courageous lay leaders who will keep them alert and open to new movements of the Spirit.

These illustrations of seasons when ministers may seek a vision by no means exhaust the possibilities. These benchmarks suggest only a few of the moments when the quest for a vision becomes urgent. When visions fade or have been fulfilled or shatter on the rocks of resistance, visionaries must seek a new vision to avoid drifting to the edges of God's movement in the world. They should remember that life along the banks of the stream will prove dull indeed in comparison to the rapid movement of the water in the channel.

The relation between spirituality and vision should not be too difficult to discern. A vision demands personal contact with God, an engagement initiated by the Lord. Although the vision-seeker feels that she is seeking God with all her soul, mind, and strength, she discovers later that she is being sought. The old hymnwriter had it right when he wrote, "I sought the Lord, and afterward I knew/He moved my soul to seek Him, seeking me."

The importance of vision in a minister has parallels for the importance of vision in lay leaders, both for their ministry in the church and their vocation in the world. Not surprisingly, what we have described as the possible pitfalls of the minister also lurk along the pathway of lay leaders. They too can become complacent in past achievements; they can become fearful of what might happen if new directions were chosen; they can fail in their call to engage and encourage the minister to lead with assertive wisdom. It is important that lay leaders be aware of these perils, because avoiding them allows them to do their essential work unhindered. Spiritual leadership requires the mutual efforts of the pastor and the lay leaders. In this mutual quest, in God's inexplicable ways, the Spirit moves over the chaotic waters churning in the human spirit and gives order, perspective, and direction. From this encounter with God, spiritual leaders go into their ministry with focus, certitude, and empowerment. They not only see the vision but also implement the vision.

Four key elements seem to define a vital spirituality. First, a hunger for God in which the soul seeks to go beyond itself. Second, an encounter with God in a manner that produces powerful vision, energy, and conviction. Third, a transformation and redirection of a leadership team. And, finally, lives of active engagement focused in a clear direction.

Aspects of Seeking a Vision

At this point it may be valuable to reflect on different aspects of seeking a vision. For leaders, the search for a vision is both personal and corporate. If a leader is without a personal vision for his life, he will find it difficult to discern a vision for the congregation. It is possible that leaders may discover their vision on their own. It is also possible that the vision for the congregation held and supported by others may awaken a vision in them. In either case, the corporate vision is grounded in a community of persons who have personal visions. We believe that a life vision has been planted in the deep levels of everyone's consciousness. If this conviction is accurate, the vision you seek is already part of you, an "original vision" written into your very being.

In addition to the vision within, we should also look at the prophetic vision. The prophet's vision most nearly matches the images that the word "vision" evokes. The prophetic vision is marked by drama, vivid pictures, and a sense of the overwhelming presence of God. When we consider the prophet's vision, Isaiah in the temple, Jeremiah in his mother's womb, and Ezekiel in the Valley of Dry Bones come to mind. What might we learn by revisiting the prophet's vision?

Along these same lines we discover the mystic's vision. Teresa of Ávila, among others, writes about spiritual visions and offers safeguards to protect against self-deception. She would probably be a good guide for anyone seeking a vision.

Finally, we believe the vision quest that is germane to Native American spirituality presents a model that compares favorably with the Christian quest. Looking at these four aspects of vision will, we believe, both stimulate and inform our search for a vision for our lives and for the church.

Kinds of Vision

Visions fall into three categories — original vision, prophetic vision, and mystic vision. An examination of each of these will open up new possibilities in our thinking or reveal to us visions long since forgotten.

The Original Vision

The primary meaning of "original vision" refers to God's vision of us. The psalmist speaks of this vision:

> For it was you who formed my inward parts; you knit me together in my mother's womb. I praise you, for I am fearfully and wonderfully made. Wonderful are your works; that I know very well. My frame was not hidden from you, when I was being made in secret, intricately woven in the depths of the earth. Your eyes beheld my unformed substance. In your book were written all the days that were formed for me, when none of them as yet existed. How weighty to me are your thoughts, O God! How vast is the sum of them! (Ps. 139:13-17)

This burst of praise from the psalmist recognizes that God saw him before he existed and began forming him from the beginning. Nothing was hidden from the penetrating and all-knowing vision of God. *"Your eyes beheld my unformed substance. In your book were written all the days that were formed for me, when none of them as yet existed."* God saw us from the moment of our creation, knew our inward parts and even how many days we would live. So the original vision is God's vision of us; God saw in an instant who we were and what we were to become. In our experience, this vision that God had of us in our creation suggests not only that we are made *by* God but that we are made *for* God.

This mark of creation has left within each of us a longing for "something more." Carl Jung, the Swiss psychiatrist, gave a prominent place to the concept of "individuation." In this concept he pointed to the drive within persons to become who they were created to be, to actualize the intention written in their psyche. To protect his scientific standing, Jung did not say that the drive for individuation was propelled by the intention of God, but he gives evidence that makes us believe that this is what he thought.

As persons of faith, we readily testify to the persistence of God's call within us, driving us toward our destiny and the fulfillment of our purpose. John Sanford, who has written extensively about Jung from a Christian perspective, simplified the explanation of this drive when he said, "There is something in us that knows who we are and what we are to become." Both Jung and Sanford are sensing God's vision of us from the beginning, a vision seeking to work itself out in the concrete circumstances of our lives.

Some of us recall the devotional writings of E. Stanley Jones, a missionary to India. In a little book entitled *The Way,* he speaks of the will of God being written into the genetic structure of our bodies. In every aspect of our life, he claims, we are made by God and for God. Jones is yet another voice echoing the claims of Jung and Sanford.

Since the original vision refers to God's vision of us, perhaps ours is a vision of God's vision of us. When in high moments of awareness we glimpse the profound meaning of our lives, what we behold is God's vision of us. Our vision, therefore, is a reflected vision, like rays of the sun bouncing off the moon.

In addition to God's vision of us and our vision of God's vision, there is yet another aspect of the original vision. "Original" in this sense refers to the temporal aspect of the vision: it is the first in a series. The first vision of our lives may come at a very early age. Yet this sense of reality, of purpose and meaning, remains in our memory and informs our whole lives. Perhaps these original visions grow out of the intention God has written into the soul. In his book entitled *The Original Vision,* Edward Robinson offers a woman's moving and revealing account of the vision she had as a young girl:

> When I was about five I had the experience on which, in a sense, my life has been based. It has always remained real and true for me. Sitting in the garden one day I suddenly became conscious of a colony of ants in the grass, running rapidly and purposefully about their business. Pausing to watch them I studied the form of their activity, wondering how much of their own pattern they were able to see for themselves. All at once I knew that I was so large that, to them, I was

70

invisible — except, perhaps, as a shadow over their lives. I was gigantic, huge — able at one glance to comprehend, at least to some extent, the work of the whole colony. . . . But they knew nothing of the earth except for the tiny part of it which was their home.

Turning away from them to my surroundings, I saw there was a tree not far away, and the sun was shining. There were clouds, and blue sky that went on for ever and ever. And suddenly I was tiny — so little and weak and insignificant that it didn't really matter at all whether I existed or not. And yet, insignificant as I was, my mind was capable of understanding that the limitless world I could see was beyond my comprehension. I could know myself to be a minute part of it all. I could understand my lack of understanding.

A watcher would have to be incredibly big to see me and the world around me as I could see the ants and their world, I thought. Would he think me to be as unaware of his existence as I knew the ants were of mine? He would have to be vaster than the world and space, and beyond understanding, and yet I *could* be aware of him — I *was* aware of him, in spite of my limitations. At the same time he was, and he was not, beyond my understanding.

Although my flash of comprehension was thrilling and transforming, I knew even then that in reality it was no more than a tiny glimmer. And yet, because there was this glimmer of understanding, the door of eternity was already open. . . .

Running indoors, delighted with my discovery, I announced happily, "We're like ants, running about on a giant's tummy!" No one understood, but that was unimportant. I knew what I knew.[1]

Here is a primal vision of God and the universe that came to a child of five years old. This vision is, according to her report, "the experience on which, in a sense, my life has been based." The analogy of God relating to her like she related to the ants shaped her vision of the world as friendly, inclusive, and stable. She returned to this vision throughout her life to find her center, her sense of direction, her security. This was indeed an original vision and a life-directing one.

1. Edward Robinson, *The Original Vision: A Study of the Religious Experience of Childhood* (New York: Seabury, 1983), pp. 12-13.

Haven't many of us had these original visions long before we reached adulthood? Haven't most of us early on had visions of God's intention for us — even though we may not have named it as something coming from God at the time? Isn't it still alive somewhere inside of us? Can we recover it and let it speak once again?

The Prophetic Vision

The biblical description of the vision of Israel's prophets also shapes our concept of vision. Nearly all the prophets of Israel received their calls in the form of visions described with compelling directness and rich symbolism. The prophets may have been following sheep, worshipping in the temple, or lamenting the exile in Babylon when the Lord God came to them. Their calls came from beyond themselves, confronted them with the presence of the Lord, and gave them a word to speak to the people. These visions led not to wealth and social ease but to testing, rejection, and sometimes death. Representing Yahweh to the people was a task that was neither easy nor safe.

Remember Jeremiah's call and the prophetic vision that accompanied it when he encountered the Lord:

> Now the word of the LORD came to me saying, "Before I formed you in the womb I knew you, and before you were born I consecrated you; I appointed you a prophet to the nations." Then I said, "Ah, Lord GOD! Truly I do not know how to speak, for I am only a boy." But the LORD said to me, "Do not say, 'I am only a boy'; for you shall go to all to whom I send you, and you shall speak whatever I command you. Do not be afraid of them, for I am with you to deliver you, says the LORD." Then the LORD put out his hand and touched my mouth; and the LORD said to me, "Now I have put my words in your mouth." (Jer. 1:4-9)

In this event the original vision of God for Jeremiah and the prophetic vision come together. The God who formed Jeremiah in his mother's womb and knew him from that moment was now the God who called him to speak to the nations. No resistance from Jeremiah could withstand the compelling call of God. God promised to send him, to give him words to speak, to give him the courage to speak them, and to deliver him.

When the debate was settled, the Almighty placed a divine hand upon Jeremiah's mouth and put his holy words on Jeremiah's lips. Jeremiah's description of his dramatic encounter with God and the call issued to him was his way of articulating his vision of the Invisible. What do you suppose the memory of this encounter meant to Jeremiah when he was cast into prison? Or when he was shamed and discounted by the people?

The Mystic Vision

Teresa of Ávila, a Carmelite nun whose life spanned most of the sixteenth century, had numerous spiritual encounters with God. Her superiors commanded her to write about these experiences, visions, and revelations, which she was reluctant to do. Throughout her writings she constantly discounts herself, commenting that she is dumb, stupid, and unable to write her thoughts clearly. Yet, when we read Teresa's writings, we are amazed at her insight and clarity of expression.

In *The Interior Castle* Teresa describes three kinds of mystical vision that will further illuminate our discussion.[2] First, she speaks of a vision of the presence of God. In this type of vision, she suggests, we do not actually see God beside us, nor do we have images of God in our minds. In her experience, this type of vision seems to be more of a sharpened awareness of the Divine Presence with us, an awareness that comes to us spontaneously. Other mystics describe this kind of vision as full of images, images generated by the presence of God rather than by human efforts. Whether image-filled or not, this kind of vision is more like a visitation beyond our control, a Presence that comes over us, rather than a result of our intentions to encounter the presence of God.

Teresa suggests that this "good Jesus" may come to us when we are least expecting his presence, at a time we have not even asked for it. Nevertheless, he comes to us, and even though we cannot see him, we know that he is there. As Teresa explains it, "[This] presence which the soul has

2. St. Teresa of Ávila, *The Interior Castle* (Garden City, N.Y.: Image Books, 1961), pp. 178-203.

at its side makes it sensitive to everything. For though we know quite well that God is present in all that we do, our nature is such that it makes us lose sight of the fact; but when this favor is granted it can no longer do so, for the Lord, who is near at hand, awakens it."[3]

Second, Teresa speaks of the imaginary vision. By this she means not "a pretended vision" but a sought-after vision that draws on the imagination. Through meditation a person focuses upon the image of Jesus. With the inspiration of Scripture, a hymn, or the Eucharist, a person forms an image of Christ, thinks about Christ, and intentionally opens himself or herself to the Divine Presence.

This intentional use of images in meditation was more fully developed by a contemporary of Teresa's, a spiritual giant to whom we have previously referred: Ignatius of Loyola. In the imaginary vision, a person meditates on an image of the presence of Jesus taken from Scripture. For example, we might focus our attention upon Jesus walking by the sea, calling disciples to follow him. As we immerse ourselves in that scene from the life of Jesus, we become aware of his presence before us, beholding us, speaking to us.

In this kind of vision, we look at the Lord so deeply that we become unaware of ourselves. This imaginary vision — unlike the unsought vision of the Presence that will last for only a short time — may linger for days or for more than a year.

Third, Teresa speaks of the intellectual vision. This vision comes to us as an insight into a profound truth about God; it is a revelation we receive through our minds. Yet, this revelation does not result from our logic or reason; it comes to us intuitively. It is unlike the mystical vision in that it does not focus our attention on the Divine Presence. It is unlike the imaginary vision because it does not depend upon our efforts. This vision comes spontaneously and lasts only a few seconds, but its effect remains for a lifetime.

When Teresa describes this experience of the Spirit, she explains that the soul sees nothing but that the experience is "a notably intellectual vision, in which is revealed to the soul how all things are seen in God, and how within Himself he contains them."[4] In the intellectual vision, God reveals a truth that is in Godself, and any truth we discover seems by

3. St. Teresa, *The Interior Castle*, p. 181.
4. St. Teresa, *The Interior Castle*, p. 194.

comparison like "thick darkness." Such a vision is highly positive, and though it passes in moments, the result remains in the soul to direct and inspire it.

When we look at the different forms of vision, we recognize that one of them resides in us (the original vision), another confronts us in our call (the prophetic vision), and the final one comes gratuitously through the grace of God (the mystic vision).

Each of these perspectives — the original vision, the prophetic vision, and the mystic vision — has something distinctive to contribute to the search for a vision for the church and for the lives of the persons who lead it.

When we think about the original vision, we see immediately that it offers a grounding in God's purpose. God has a purpose for every church, and it is quite simple: to re-present Jesus Christ to the world and to be an agent of the kingdom. Jesus defined this purpose through his life and teaching, and it continues to be expressed through the work of his Spirit. The leaders' task must always be to discern what aspect of Christ's person and ministry seems appropriate to emphasize in a particular time and place.

From time to time, God confronts the church with the prophetic vision to awaken it to its calling. So often warring forces pull the church first one way and then another. A particular church may at one point so completely identify with the culture that it is powerless, then become so focused on its purity of dogma that it becomes irrelevant. Or, at various times in its life, a church might focus so intently upon education or spirituality or church growth that it upsets the balance of these important aspects of its life. When these excesses occur, the Lord of the Church sends a prophet with a vision to issue a call to change. The prophetic vision renounces the status quo and sets forth a vision of "newness" that is seldom welcomed but always necessary.

The mystic vision, in all its aspects, draws the church closer to an encounter with the Holy. True, the original vision has its origin in God and has a way of continually pressing its call upon the church. And, of course, the prophetic vision results in Godspeech to the church. But the mystic vision gives a sense of being overcome — even invaded — by the Divine Presence.

The way of the mystic vision, like the other two approaches, has what we might call "vague edges." Nevertheless, what the mystic vision brings to the visioning process is critical. The mystic vision invites church leaders to a sharpened awareness of the presence of Christ in their lives and in their imaginations. It especially calls leaders to pay attention to the images, insights, and inspirations they receive with respect to the mission of the church. As these come into consciousness, they are to be honored and attended. Following the cue of both Teresa and Ignatius, leaders can place themselves in the presence of Christ, bring their needs to him, and heed the vision that the living Lord inspires in them. At its core the vision is a face-to-face encounter with God. Visions born in this encounter will change the manner in which we "do church" by adding a depth and authenticity lacking in many congregations.

The Vision Quest

Although the vision cannot be discovered, demanded, or self-induced, it is possible for us to follow our yearnings, prepare ourselves for a vision, and expect God to reveal Godself to us. The form of the vision quest is not a new phenomenon to those who seek God. Jesus' forty days in the wilderness constituted a quest for the vision of his life. Elijah went on a vision quest in the wilderness after he defeated the prophets of Baal. Pastors and laypersons today who face enormous challenges, weighty decisions, and new opportunities often leave their routines to find solace and search for a vision of their lives.

To the best of our knowledge, no one has detailed the vision quest as fully as Native Americans have. All North American tribes believe in the vision quest; it lies at the heart of Native American spirituality. In exploring this ritual, we have found Kathleen Margaret Dugan's book entitled *The Vision Quest of the Plains Indians* to be extremely helpful.

Although the quest is shrouded in mystery, the method of pursuit can be outlined. The vision quest begins with an unshakable conviction that an invisible presence exists and can and will answer every need if approached in the right way. But in their practice of the quest, Native Americans made certain that the presence of the Spirit was free and acted according to its own will.

76

Generally speaking, the person seeking the vision feels a deep need for assistance. This need arises out of a variety of circumstances. A person may undertake a quest to gain courage to face a coming crisis or a difficult ordeal. Or he or she may seek a favor from the Great Spirit (or, on occasion, seek to give thanks for a gift received). Often the quest is a confession of the seeker's need to find direction for his or her life. Sometimes the seeker may want help in understanding a vision that he or she has received unexpectedly. Whatever the reason for the pursuit of the quest, the desire to undertake it is considered a call from the Great Spirit.

The person seeking a vision first finds a holy person who gives instruction in the pursuit of the vision, or alternatively consults with the tribe. The vision quest cannot begin without the consent and direction of a holy person or the tribe.

In preparation for the quest, the seeker searches out a place, usually a high, secluded place. At the outset the seeker strips off most of his clothes as an act of humility and vulnerability. In this almost-naked state, the seeker marks the boundaries of the place, clears it of all living things, and invokes the four winds not to bring inclement weather.

At an early stage in the quest, the seeker cries out to the Great Spirit, humbling himself both verbally and emotionally by confessing his ignorance and need. The vision seeker "remembers his nothingness in the presence of the Great Spirit."[5] After making this confession of "nothingness," the seeker waits for the vision, meditating continuously upon the quest. The seeker invokes the Great Spirit, verbally or mentally, in song and in prayer. He may stand or sit, be awake or asleep, but he must not leave the space prepared for the quest. He also must not eat or drink while making the quest. The vision may come to him at any time, whether he is awake or asleep. It may come in the form of anything that breathes — an animal, perhaps — or it may come through an inanimate object. The vision may communicate itself in several ways — in unintelligible speech, in strange words, or in the language of birds and beasts. However strange it may seem, the vision will make itself known as the vision being sought. The seeker must wait until the vision comes, however long that may be. Sometimes, having reached the point of exhaustion, he gives up.

5. Kathleen Margaret Dugan, *The Vision Quest of the Plains Indians: Its Spiritual Significance* (Lewiston, N.Y.: The Edwin Mellen Press, 1985), p. 133.

If the seeker receives a vision, he must announce it to a gathering of the tribe or to a holy person in private. The vision is never intended just for the individual seeker; it is meant for the whole tribe. Perhaps this explains why those who receive a vision must report them to the community or to responsible leaders for discernment and confirmation.

Those who have made fruitful quests return changed persons. The experience of the quest seems to rearrange their dispositions and priorities. Quietness may become more important than self-assertion, for example. And the character of the recipients seems to be transformed too. (Not surprisingly, it is generally only those of exemplary character who receive visions.) The visions empower the seekers and give them a sense of how to accomplish what they have learned.

We know of a few congregations that have begun to offer Christian vision quests for their young people as they move from their teen years to adulthood. In one of these congregations, the quest begins with an extended time of formation and education. During this time, adult members of the congregation help prepare the young people for fasting, safety in the wilderness, extended times of prayer and meditation, and the interior rigors of solitude. In addition, they share their faith with the youth, passing on the wisdom of the congregation, the congregation's myth. This passing on of faith includes a time when adult members tell the stories of their spiritual lives, sharing their questions, fears, joys, and assurances, offering the truths that have sustained them, and repeating the Scripture passages that have nourished and challenged them. After this period of preparation, the young people gather at a Sunday-morning worship service and are sent out with the blessings and prayers of the congregation.

During the quest, which is held in a fairly remote place, adult guides and a number of youth who have not felt called to the full vision quest are stationed in a nearby "base camp" to support the seekers with a presence of safety and prayer. After five days — including three days of solitary fasting and prayer — the young people return to be welcomed by the congregation during a Sunday-morning worship service. At that time they share with the congregation the experience of their quest. The congregation affirms this experience and helps them see the ways it may or may not connect with the congregation's existing vision. Through the process of the vision quest, the youth not only receive the wisdom, faith, and blessing handed down from their elders, but they begin to identify and embrace the original visions in their own lives. By embracing these visions, they can begin to respond more fully to God's invitation for their lives as individuals and as members of a community of faith. In addition, the congregation shifts or expands its vision as it receives something new.

Here are the key things leaders need to know about the vision quest:

1. Those who find themselves facing a crisis or in the midst of one should seek a vision.
2. A vision quest should not be undertaken lightly and should have the blessing of those whom we trust.
3. Proper preparation and guidance should be sought before making the quest.
4. The choice and preparation of a place is important to the success of the quest.
5. The quest made by an individual or a group should be marked by a sense of urgency and persistence.
6. Those seeking the vision should be open to whatever way in which God chooses to speak to them.
7. The vision that is received must be taken back to the host community, shared with them, and incorporated into the broader vision of the community.

May the Lord guide you as you go about the urgent task of seeking a vision for the church and for your own life.

QUESTIONS FOR REFLECTION AND DISCUSSION

1. What is your vision for your congregation and for your own life? What is your original vision?
2. What do you see in the description of the prophetic vision that has relevance for the church today?
3. What aspects of the mystic vision challenge you?
4. How do you think the vision quest might be valuble for the church today?

SUGGESTIONS FOR JOURNALING

1. On a sheet of paper draw a lifeline with "birth" at the bottom and "now" at the top.
2. Begin with your earliest memory and review your various visions. Write a word or phrase along the points of the lifeline that will identify each one.
3. Choose one of these visions and describe it as fully as you can recall it.
4. Write a prayer that flows naturally out of this recalling of the visions of your life.
5. Pray to the Lord for a vision for your congregation.

Chapter Six

THE IMPORTANCE OF
SPIRITUAL COMPANIONSHIP

Members in the Church of Jesus Christ yearn for spiritual friendship and guidance today more than at any other time in recent history. Yet many churches seem unable to meet their spiritual needs. Note how many of them have turned to New Age spirituality or have looked outside their own church for help with their spiritual journeys. We think there are specific reasons for this blight on the life of mainline churches, and that it can be treated with appropriate responses.

The need is clearly illustrated in a recent experience of a professor at a theological seminary. Diane, a recent graduate who was now pastoring a church, called for an appointment to see him. She didn't say what the visit was about, but she kept her appointment promptly.

When she entered the office of her former professor, she said, "Lately you seem to be everywhere. I see your name in the seminary publication; I go to a luncheon, and you are the speaker; I get a brochure in the mail, and it describes a program you've started. Your name keeps coming up again and again. What does this mean? What's going on here?"

"What do you think?" the professor responded.

In somewhat the same tongue-in-cheek manner, Diane continued: "Am I getting too near the edge? Am I about to go off the deep end? I don't know what's happening to me. Is God at work, or what?"

"What else is happening that brings you to these questions?" the professor asked.

"Well, several things are happening in our church. We have this small group of people who on their own have begun to read the Bible, pray, and share their lives with each other. Things are happening to them that they don't understand. They're asking me questions about God, but the correct theological answers don't satisfy them. I know they're asking for more than I'm giving them."

The old friend nodded and smiled as he motioned her to go on.

"At the request of some of these 'newly awakened' people, we've changed our Wednesday-evening family gathering. Each week we're asking one person to talk about his or her experience of God. After that person finishes, we ask for prayer requests. These requests have become serious — they're about people with cancer, couples facing divorce, sick children, and other issues just as crucial. And these folks are expecting us to pray for them as if we truly believe our prayers will be answered."

Realizing that the conversation was getting deeper and more involved for the former student, the old professor remained silent, letting the truth of what the young minister said sink in.

"And another thing," she said. "We have this woman who's married to a Jewish man, and they have a fourteen-year-old son. The mixed marriage is working well, but the son had some type of disease the doctors couldn't diagnose. They treated him for Lou Gehrig's disease, but he kept getting worse. One Wednesday evening after the prayer service, this woman came into my office and asked me if I could pray for him. And I did pray. I summoned all my faith and prayed for him to be healed."

"And?" the professor prompted.

"They took him to another doctor who diagnosed him with Lyme disease. He's being treated for it, and he's going to get well. What am I to make of this? Was my prayer literally answered? Am I going crazy? Am I getting too far out?"

"No, you're not going crazy, and you're not getting too far out. The Spirit of God has begun doing new things among mainline churches, making innovations not of their own choosing. Perhaps this is part of God's new work for today."

Then the young woman said, "You know that I wasn't taught this in seminary. Nobody ever taught me to talk about my experience of God, or how to listen to people who were having strange things like I've described happen to them."

"No," the old man agreed. "You came to us at a time when we had given up on the free and spontaneous movement of the Spirit and the immediacy of the Divine Presence with us."

"What should I do?" she asked with painful earnestness.

"I think it might be helpful for you to have a spiritual guide," he said.

"What's that?" she asked.

"You find someone with whom you can meet on a regular basis — say, once a month — to talk with about what God is doing in your life. This relationship will help you be accountable and keep you focused."

"What's it like?"

"Something like what you and I have been doing for the last half-hour. You meet, spend time in silence together, talk about what's going on in your life with God, and pray. The spiritual friend will try to help you notice things in your life that otherwise might go unattended."

"I've heard of that kind of a relationship, but I've never been engaged in one."

"Diane, for the entire time that we've been talking, a name has been coming to my mind. I think you would benefit from seeing Janice Green."

Diane almost jumped out of her chair when the professor said the name. "I knew it — I knew you were going to say Janice's name before it even came out of your mouth. I was with her during a conference two weeks ago, and she asked me to lunch last week. And all the time we were eating, I kept wondering, 'Why am I here? Why am I talking with Janice Green?' Is that a coincidence, or what?"

Two things seem to emerge from this conversation between a recent graduate and a sensitive professor. First, the Spirit of God is acting upon mainline congregations in new and fresh ways. Second, many church leaders don't know how to embrace this movement of the Spirit and nurture it. In many of our congregations there are persons like those involved in the small group in Diane's church who have encountered the presence of the Spirit and are seeking to be receptive to what God is doing in their lives. There are no patterns to the Spirit's work, but new life and energy seem to be aborning. Pastors and lay leaders often don't know what to make of these manifestations of the Spirit and tend to respond more with fear than gratitude. We wonder if this dilemma is the result of an Enlightenment-imbued culture and a theological seminary whose training long ago gave up on the Spirit. Given this large omission in the seminary training of pastors, we should not be surprised at both the ignorance and the hunger of the laity.

Needed: Another Dimension of Leadership

Congregations are calling upon their pastors and lay leaders for a kind of ministry that their leaders have not previously considered or been equipped for. Effective leaders in today's church are being called upon to engage persons in their journey and speak with them about the issues of living in the presence of Christ.

Those leaders who provide effective leadership become doctor, midwife, and friend to persons who are beginning to awaken to the Spirit. On the spiritual path, life changes, and newness begins to appear. A new person, the person God is longing for, is being formed.

In this new call to ministry, leaders will need to serve as doctors who help treat the diseases of the soul, those afflictions that stifle the soul's progress. Some people will need this treatment in order to get on with their journey; others will need it before they can seriously begin their journey.

Often leaders will refer persons to therapists and/or medical professionals, and continue to monitor their progress. For instance, the individual who is suffering the ravages of untreated clinical depression may be unable to make progress on the spiritual path. He or she simply may not have the emotional and physical resources to summon the degree of focused intention and deliberate attention necessary for the rigors of the journey. Depression needs therapeutic attention, but it may well involve a physiological component that needs professional medical attention as well.

At the same time, there may also be a spiritual component to the depression that requires theological sensitivity. Suppose, for instance, that a young woman suffers from depression because as a child she was abused by a neighbor and feels guilt or shame. While a therapist may offer psychological and emotional help, and a medical professional may offer help in alleviating any related physiological dysfunction, who will help her recover a sense of God not tainted by the godlike figure that abused her as a child? Here the spiritually alive church has a responsibility in the healing task. It can help this person renew her capacity to receive the God of love, and it can offer her this love.

When a person is healthy enough to receive God's love, new possibilities open up for her: she may recognize that she longs for a deeper intimacy with God. At this point the spiritual companion's role becomes more like that of a midwife. Margaret Guenther, writing about spiritual direction in her book entitled *Holy Listening*, paints a profound picture of this role.[1] Traditionally, the midwife is a woman whose experience in bearing children allows her to guide other women in giving birth. The midwife knows the movements, both positive and negative, of the birthing process, understands what will make things go more smoothly, and can offer suggestions and encouragement at the right times. She takes her cues from the one who is giving birth, watching and listening for hints of what is being born. But she does not know what new life will come. She is awaiting the mystery of that new life, helping to coax it into existence.

The spiritual leader plays a similar role with the seeking soul. The leader sees in the life of the seeker a new person trying to be born anew or enlivened by the Spirit. Will this new being live or die? What will it look like? How strong will it be? All these questions evidence the presence of mystery, even to one as experienced as the midwife. So, like a midwife, the spiritual leader make no demands upon the new life. The leader's agenda calls only for helping this new life come into being, breathe deeply, and unfold in whatever form God has in mind.

When a new life in God has matured for a time, seems to be flourishing in the Spirit, and is drinking deeply from the Well, the role of the spiritual guide may shift. Now something like a "soul friendship" can develop. As a soul friend, the leader may be less of a guide or a coach than a companion on the way.

Journeying together on the path that this person has chosen, both the leader and the friend will pass the same sights, but perhaps the leader will see them from a different perspective. The friend will point to something and describe what he sees. Although the leader may be more experienced in the spiritual life, she will see sights she's seen before, but now with new eyes and from a different angle. Her tasks are to help her friend notice these

1. Margaret Guenther, *Holy Listening: The Art of Spiritual Direction* (Boston: Cowley Publications, 1992), pp. 82-108.

sights ("Wait a minute. See that? Let's look at it for a while.") and to listen for what he sees there ("What does that look like to you?"). The leader will also encourage deeper exploration ("Why don't we go closer so we can get a better look?"), and will offer her own perspective when it seems appropriate ("I notice how warm it is here."). The leader as spiritual friend, like the midwife, surrenders her own agendas to God and keeps trying to pay attention to what God has in store for the one she accompanies on the way.

Up to this point we have been describing the spiritual leader's relationship with individuals. But leaders can play similar roles with the congregation as a whole. Whether you are the pastor or an established leader, you can see the congregation as a corporate body; you can think of it in the same way you do a person, an individual body.

It is important to remember that the congregation may need healing before it has the capacity to receive God's love and fruitfully commit itself to the spiritual journey. As spiritual leaders, your task will be to identify the disease that weakens your congregation's health and help marshal the resources necessary to relieve its dysfunction.

All of us who are leaders must avoid the temptation to drag our congregation onto the path before it is able to make the journey. We need to realize that too much of our own agenda can get mixed up with the growth and spiritual development of our congregations. We are plagued by an interior voice reminding us that we gave our time and effort to Christ in the first place to bring congregations to life spiritually. We live in secret fear that the spiritual health of our congregations is an extension of our own spiritual health. Such insecurities can lead us to overlook the true situation of our congregations, to focus on where we want them to go rather than on where they are. Seeing them where they are may involve recognizing that they first need a doctor to heal their wounds.

When the "person" that is your congregation has developed the capacity to receive God's love, you may become the midwife that helps it give birth. And as it matures in the spiritual life, you will become its soul friend, accompanying it on the way. For the moment we want only to note these similarities between the individual and the congregation. But in order to develop the capacities of a soul friend, it is important to take a hard look at what is happening within your own soul. For if we do not know the movements of our own souls, we will be blind to the movements of God in the souls of others.

Needed: Spiritual Guidance for Leaders

In their spiritual development, many lay leaders and clergy have followed similar paths with corresponding consequences. The lay leaders of many congregations were reared in the church and attended church school, youth fellowship, church camps, and work camps that involved helping families in need. They were "churched" from preschool through high school, and after they attended college, many of them came back to participate actively in the life of the church. Because they were children of the church who attended regularly and gave generously, they were made officials in the church. No one would question that these are good persons who care about the values emphasized in the church.

The ministers of these congregations may have backgrounds similar to those of the lay leaders, except that they have attended seminary for three years. During those three years they studied the Bible, the history of the church, theology, and the skills of preaching, teaching, and pastoral care. In most cases they graduated from seminary with a love for the church and a genuine desire to do good in the world.

Many lay leaders and clergy are alike in that they have had significant religious experiences but have not received intentional spiritual formation. The local congregations assumed that participation in the life of the church would properly equip lay leaders, and seminaries assumed that pastors would be properly equipped for spiritual leadership by participating in church life and attending seminary. We think that assumption has been shown to be inaccurate.

The deficiency of church and seminary experience in forming persons in the faith can be easily illustrated with a single example. A bright, talented young woman was in her second year of training in a particular seminary. When she was interviewed as part of her mid-course assessment, she was asked questions about faith, life, the call, and future decisions she might make. When the review committee was discussing her responses, one of the professors who was new to the institution said, "I was surprised that this person didn't seem comfortable using theological language to describe her life experiences." Immediately her comment was met with an explanation from the chair of her assessment committee: "Well, she has been reared in the church and attended our camps, and I'm sure she knows the language quite well."

87

If she knew it, why didn't she use it?

We are certain that leaders of the church have had numerous spiritual experiences while worshiping, preaching, preparing sermons, serving on committees, being liturgists, reading the Bible, and doing a host of other things. What each of them has probably lacked has been the guidance of a spiritually sensitive person who could reflect with them on these experiences and give them an opportunity to verbalize their sense of the presence of God in them. When the Bible and theology are taught in a manner that not only conveys the knowledge in the tradition but also confronts the students — whether in the congregation or in the seminary — with the truth and helps them appropriate it into their lives, ministers and lay leaders will be able to articulate their faith in language their congregation will understand. When leaders in the church begin reflecting on their lives with an eye toward discovering the presence of God embedded in their narratives, they will be able to talk with others about God and assist them in their journeys.

Many leaders who have difficulty engaging brothers and sisters spiritually are not lacking spiritual experience but spiritual formation. This formation is not mysterious, nor is it difficult to engage in. But it does require that they take the time to reflect on their experiences in the light of God's purpose and presence being manifested in their lives. A clear perspective on this spiritual development will assist them in their ministry.

The Dimensions of Spiritual Development

As a spiritual leader, you need a way of thinking about where persons are on their journey with Christ — and that includes you. Without some guideposts along the way, you can easily become confused about your own journey as well as about how to help others in theirs. So in this section we want to offer a way to look at the development of the Christian spiritual life to assist you both in clarifying your own formation and in helping others on their journey.

We need to remember, of course, that some folks — even if they are living apparently good and wholesome lives — simply are not conscious of being on any kind of spiritual journey. Don't we all have moments — and sometimes months, maybe even years — like that? When we grow numb spiritually, we are unaware of anything beyond the concerns of daily living — getting through the day, making money, caring for the kids, going to church, cleaning the house, doing our tasks well, and being good citizens.

But at some point we may begin to wonder if there is more to life than the routine of living according to our own plans and energies. Again and again in the Gospels, the people who come to Jesus are turning this corner in their lives, recognizing that there might be something more to life than aimlessly following the routine. Zacchaeus climbs a tree to see Jesus. Nicodemus creeps through the darkness of night to visit him. An unnamed woman presses through a crowd to touch Jesus' cloak. Another woman braves a gathering of men to anoint Jesus' head with perfume.

At turning points such as these, new dimensions of the spiritual life begin to emerge. Over the centuries, Christian writers have identified these dimensions in a variety of ways. For effective clergy and lay leadership, we want to offer a picture of movement in the spiritual life that draws on concepts presented by Ann and Barry Ulanov in their book entitled *Primary Speech: A Psychology of Prayer.* These authors present us with five dimensions of the journey: naming the desire, naming God, naming the relationship with God, waiting, and receiving.

Naming Our Desire

The spiritual life begins with desire — a desire for God and for the expression of God in our lives and the world in forms like compassion, healing, justice, understanding, and love. Our desire for God flows from God's desire for us. At first the experience of the desire may be a vague feeling that all is not right. Or it may be misplaced desire — a hunger for material things, for instance, that fail to satisfy us. But if we notice the awakening of our desire and pay attention to it, the path into the Divine Mystery will begin to open before us. Yes, God knows our deepest longings, but God also wants us to know them. And God wants us to be specific about our desire. Only then can we make progress on our spiritual journey.

Recall how Jesus asked Bartimaeus, the blind beggar from Jericho, "What do you want me to do for you?" Wasn't it obvious? Perhaps! But

Bartimaeus needed to know himself as intimately as Jesus knew him. He needed to acknowledge the fact that he longed for something more than having someone lead him to the next corner or buy him lunch or help him pick out his clothes. He needed to confess with his lips, "Let me see again!" That was his deepest desire. Only by naming it could his healing begin.

The story of the Samaritan woman at the well, which we read in John 4, also shows us the importance of recognizing our deepest desire. In fact, in her story we see all the phases of a lifetime's spiritual journey compressed into a few days. But these phases appear only in bits and pieces, emerging with complexity and subtlety, just as they do in real life.

Picture this woman as an awareness of her deepest desire begins to dawn on her. What must she have felt? What responses would she have had? We must read between the lines in this story, but don't we have to read between the lines of the stories of people in our congregations, too? Ministering to the spiritual needs of persons demands this kind of imaginative hermeneutics.

Before the Samaritan woman met Jesus, her desire had been misplaced, scattered across the bedrooms of her many husbands. But then Jesus' words crystallize her fragmented desire into a strong thirst for a new kind of water. As her desire surfaces, she struggles to understand it. At first she thinks it has to do only with physical things — never needing a drink of water again, never having to traipse to the well again. But in conversation with Jesus, the nature of the water she desires begins to become clearer. If we could ask her to name it, perhaps she would speak of a profound intimacy, of being completely known for who she is — and to be loved in the knowing. Sexual relationships with five men have been unable to satisfy that desire for deep intimacy. But this stranger seems to know her more intimately than she knows herself. As she begins to grasp this deeper vision of herself, her life changes.

When we encounter someone who has not yet uncovered her own desire, we may be tempted to tell her what we think she is longing for. We want so much for her to know God's way; we want her to catch sight of what we think we see. But what does Jesus do with the Samaritan woman? He simply describes her life to her. He tells her the situation: "You have had five husbands." Then he lets her draw her own connections. The way in which he deals with this woman is but another way of saying, "What do you want me to do for you?" Jesus knows that if her desire is deep enough, she will enter into it herself. True change will come for her only if she finds the way herself, understands her own deepest desire. And so, as understanding dawns, she is able to move to the next phase: discovering her name for God.

Perhaps it would be helpful for your own formation if at this point you paused and asked yourself, "What is my deepest desire?" When you have named it, push yourself a bit harder: "Is this truly my deepest desire?" As you begin to reflect on this question, you can also ask, "What do I desire for my life? What do I desire for other members in the church? What do I desire for the congregation as a whole?"

Naming God

As we come to know our deepest desires, our deepest selves, we come to know something of God. God is the answer to our deepest desires. In this phase of the journey, we get a glimpse of the nature of God through the window of our self. John Calvin put it like this in his opening to the *Institutes*:

> Without knowledge of self there is no knowledge of God. Nearly all the wisdom we possess, that is to say, true and sound wisdom, consists of two parts: the knowledge of God and of ourselves. But, while joined by many bonds, which one precedes and brings forth the other is not easy to discern. In the first place, no one can look upon himself without immediately turning his thoughts to the contemplation of God, in whom he "lives and moves."[2]

Calvin and other great Christian writers have recognized that God meets us as we are, ministers to us in the place where our need is greatest, accommodates the Divine Presence to us humans. Do we desire guidance? Perhaps God is our Wonderful Counselor. Do we need comfort and security? Maybe our name for God is Shepherd. Do we lack companionship? God may be Friend to us. Are we confused? God comes to us as Wisdom.

2. John Calvin, *The Institutes of the Christian Religion* (Philadelphia: Westminster Press, 1960), I, i, p. 35.

As the Samaritan woman begins to understand the nature of her own desire, she tries on names for the Holy Presence before her. She has desired to be intimately known, and this person seems to know her. In disclosing her to herself, he has met her deepest desire. What kind of person knows what others cannot? "Prophet" is the first name she gives him. He is her personal prophet, one who speaks the truth about her life, who knows the unknowable.

As we seek to name our deepest desire, we also will be naming God. As spiritual leaders our task will be to support persons who are trying to name their hunger and consequently to name the God who is manifest in that hunger. They may feel fearful or blocked or resistant; the baggage they have carried through life can hinder their calling out to God, naming God as the subject of their hunger.

But eventually the name will come. It will rise unbidden out of their longing. They know this name in the deepest recesses of their souls. It cannot and should not be forced, however. When their desire has been awakened, the name will come spontaneously. We must be there to hear it and speak it back to them. In this way they will keep trying it on like a new garment, until they reach the point where the slightest calling of the name invokes God's presence with a fullness they have not experienced before.

Before seriously considering helping another name God as the subject of their desire, reflect on your own deepest desire and the God implied in your hunger. When ministers and leaders in the church explore their own hungers and the God they long for, it prepares them to help others. Most of us have found it difficult to teach when we have not done our own homework. What does your desire evoke? What kind of God will come to meet that desire? What image of God appears to you? Or what sense of God's presence do you have? Speak to the God who comes to you. What name do you speak?

Naming Our Relationship with God

The second phase of our journey may be naming God as our deepest yearning, but soon that gives way to naming our relationship with God. For the Samaritan woman, "Prophet" soon becomes too limiting a designation for her developing relationship with Christ. She finds the need for a new name, a name that describes not herself or the little she now knows about God, but the relationship that is growing between them.

Frequently people on the spiritual path mistakenly think they have reached spiritual maturity once they have discovered their intimate name for God. Put another way, they think the name they first call God fully defines God. And since it seems they now know who God is, they can remain with this hastily defined God for the remainder of their lives. Some also mistakenly believe that everyone else must also use their name for God, and this name alone. But the name they have discovered is only the first hint of who God may be for them and for others.

This name, as we have said, describes who God seems to be for them at a particular time and place in their lives. If they keep an open heart in the exploration of the relationship, they will find that much more of God awaits them. As God meets their initial desire, they will find that God is greater than they first assumed. They will recognize that the God they have come to know is merely a pale shadow of the Creator of the universe. And they will discover that their initial relationship with God rests in the projection of their own desire.

Perhaps this path was the necessary way, even a gift from God, something not to be avoided. After all, it was through this projection of their desire that they encountered God. Now, however, it is time to explore the greatness of God beyond this highly individualized and personalized image. Very soon in their spiritual journey, seekers must recognize that the name they have given God says more about them than it does about God. With this recognition comes an important shift in the spiritual life.

This shift is visible in the story of the Samaritan woman. She moves from naming Christ her personal Prophet — the one who meets her desire, heals her wound — to a new, more expansive understanding. The shift happens in the space of four brief verses, a compressed account of what usually happens on our own spiritual journeys. Still, the movement is the same.

By the time she returns to the city (leaving behind the burdensome water jar that defined her old life), she is asking a new question: "He cannot be the Messiah, can he?" The story does not tell us what happened on her journey. We are left to fill in the blanks. But we know that, at the very least, her own desire is no longer defining who Christ is. Having her desire met has released her from a God of her own projection. In some way she has come to understand that God is larger than her desire, larger than she can define by a name that rises from her desire. She has recognized that her experience of God contains both who she is and who God is beyond her. In her walk to the city, perhaps she has begun to explore the surprising relationship that developed at the well. So now she is exploring a new name that speaks of a deeper and more expansive relationship with Jesus. That is how "Messiah" crosses her mind.

As leaders in the church, you should pause and consider how your focus has shifted from self-centered naming to a deepening relationship with God. What does your relationship with God look like? What name can you give it? What new thing do you discover about yourself when you attend to your relationship with God? What new thing do you discover about God? How has God become more than one who meets your desires?

Waiting for God

Waiting constitutes much of our life with God. Serious life with God is not made for those who want instant resolution and gratification. Most who have become friends of God discover that God's calendar and theirs seldom match. It seems that God has an eternity to fulfill the divine plan and thus seldom seems in a rush. How unlike most of us!

Consider again the woman at the well. She has come to the well every day to draw water. Her thirst for "something more" has lurked in her heart for a long, long time. She has waited and waited beyond all expectation. Finally, on a day like any other day, a stranger engages her in a conversation that changes her life.

Then she begins to ponder her experience. She sees it in a new light. She changes the language she uses for it. She returns to her home with hope, anticipation, and questions. "Is he the Messiah? What does it mean that he has told me about my life? Will he return? Will others also go to him and find new life?" Now another time of waiting begins, the waiting for transformation, the waiting for the new seed to grow in her and in others. What will come of this encounter?

For those of us who are leaders in the church, waiting also takes two forms. First, we wait for the fulfillment of our own desires and our own hungers. Being aware of them and naming them does not result in automatic fulfillment. So we wait for the fulfillment of our life with God. We wait for the moment when we will sense the touch of God's newness in our lives.

Second, we also wait on God for the fulfillment and transformation of ourselves and those with whom we work and for whom we pray. Experiencing the touch of newness does not engender instant transformation. And we must remember that we wait not only for moments of enlightenment and inspiration but also for lives gradually transformed. Like the woman at the well, we will find that our waiting will include some type of proclamation, some way of actively embracing the new life that has been born in us. But we continue to hold ourselves in the expectation that even more of God's grace will unfold.

Much of our spiritual life and ministry is waiting! May we do it with patience and wisdom.

Receiving God

How do we receive God? This is a very important question. Perhaps it would help us to think about receiving God in three different ways, though these are not exhaustive. Sometimes we receive God through the Word of God spoken to us. The woman at the well said, "When Messiah comes, he will proclaim all things to us." Jesus said to her, "I am he, the one who is speaking to you." Sometimes one of God's servants speaks the Word in such a manner that we know it is for us.

At other times God comes to us when our lives are in chaos and confusion. Often it takes this kind of breaking up of old arrangements for us to be able to see God at work. Regrettably, this shaking of the foundations of our lives often comes during times of tragedy or great loss. But when our old ways crumble, we may glimpse the presence of God through the brokenness.

At still other times, God may send someone into our lives with good news for us. We have no idea who this person will be, but in one of our dark hours, she will come to us and speak God's healing words. It is not difficult to imagine that the woman at the well was such a person for others. She had received God herself, welcomed God through the love of

Jesus. As part of that receiving, she was changed. God was now forming her in a new way. She began to proclaim what she had found. Though she freely admitted that she did not fully understand this mystery, she called other people to it. And she in turn became the vessel by which others received God.

How can we, as spiritual leaders, be such vessels? How can we respond to the spiritual needs of those under our care? A letter that we received from a woman not long ago illustrates clearly how this can happen.

She began by explaining that the past year had been a particularly difficult one for her. "My husband and I purchased a small restaurant in our town. We had all the hopes and dreams that go along with owning a 'family-run business.' However, things quickly started to unravel as more and more competition opened around us, and we found ourselves in a very serious financial crisis." At about the same time, the woman's mother was diagnosed with Alzheimer's disease, and she was told that her mother needed to be put in a nursing facility immediately. Needless to say, the woman felt as if her world was falling apart.

It was during this chaotic period that she visited a church in her area — an ironic event that marked the beginning of her spiritual journey. She explains in her letter: "Last fall I entered the doors of First Church for the first time, and this was after having lived in this town for eighteen years. I had vowed I would never go to that church because it was the 'popular,' 'social' place to go. I was quite sure it wasn't for me. But to my amazement something happened that Sunday that convinces me that my life has been divinely led. I am a controlling person, but, try as I might, I could never have orchestrated the events that have transpired in my life."

That Sunday in November, the minister preached in a manner that really spoke to her. He invited the congregation to risk walking with God. "At the end of the service," the woman wrote, "when he invited anyone who felt the need to talk about risking walking with God to remain and talk with the associate minister, I knew I had to do it. With tears streaming down my face, I waited to speak with her about the crises in my life and not knowing where to turn. I was totally out of character being that vulnerable."

Strangely enough, she knew the associate minister. She had been a preschool teacher before she and her husband had opened their restaurant, and this woman's daughter had been in her preschool classroom.

96

The associate minister asked her if she would be willing to have one of the lay ministers in the church visit with her. How could she resist?

Then came the next strange coincidence: "When this spiritually sensitive lay minister contacted me from the church, I was not all surprised about who it was. She was another person whose daughter I had taught in preschool."

The woman went on to describe what had happened since then:

> My talks with the lay person in the church have evolved from help in a time of crisis to a deep spiritual companionship. I know, beyond a shadow of a doubt, that God called me through this person to finally come home.
>
> I am beginning to sense something miraculous is happening here, that God can call me, not just theologians or more churchly people. My spiritual journey has intensified since [I began] talking to this deeply dedicated lay woman. It is a new and often-unfamiliar path I am walking with her, and within the safety of this cherished relationship I am able to reveal my true "imperfect" self. It is in this vulnerability that I am starting to realize God has been sustaining me, especially in the dark corners of my life, that God is trying to show me how much I am truly loved. But it took these crises in my life to pull all the props out from under me. When I finally turned toward God, God called me to be in partnership.
>
> The crises that started all of this are still in my life. Our business continues to fail, and my mother's confusion progresses at a rapid rate. Yet, I am finding a center, a peace, and joyous anticipation of what my life can be. God is sending his messengers to hold my hand along this spiritual road. He is calling me — it is the only way I can possibly describe what has been unfolding in my life over the past four months.

This woman's experience illustrates the two points we have been making: (1) that leaders in the church should have a spiritual ministry to the people of God, and (2) that the people to whom they minister generally enter into a relationship with God and deepen that relationship through a process of unfolding awareness and transformation. Notice that when this woman came to church, she heard something that awakened her desire or connected with a desire she had not named. How the preaching of the Word of God connects with an individual in this way is a mystery, but it happens again and again. In response to an invitation to risk a life with God, she began to form a name for the desire she felt. After going forward and talking with the associate minister, the initial stage of the relationship began. Then she was asked to receive a visit from one of the laity in the church, so she went home and waited. Through the sensitivity of this layperson, the woman who was burdened with problems and consumed by hungers entered into a personal relationship with God.

We believe that this woman's experience illustrates the importance of our thesis: those of us who are leaders in the church need to be able to offer spiritual companionship to those persons who come to us seeking. The outlining of the stages of movement in the spiritual life offers one explanation of the process that helps us listen with greater discernment to the searching hearts of those who come to us.

QUESTIONS FOR REFLECTION AND DISCUSSION

1. What is a spiritual companion? What role does the spiritual companion play with another person?
2. What spiritual connection do you make with the two women described in this chapter?
3. Name each of the stages in a relationship with God and explain how you connect with each of these.
4. Describe an experience in which you've had a spiritual companion.

SUGGESTIONS FOR JOURNALING

1. In your imagination, picture the first significant relationship you had with another person. Beginning with that person, make a list of the persons whom God has used in the shaping of your life spiritually.
2. Deliberately recall each of the persons on your list. Picture them. Think about the gift they gave you through your relationship with them.
3. Choose one of these persons and write a few paragraphs about them, explaining what they offered you and your feelings about them.
4. Review your list once again and "wonder" why God placed these persons in your life at the particular time they were significant to you. Note your wonderment in your journal.

Chapter Seven

THE PRACTICE OF DISCERNMENT

In the biblical sense, discernment always involves a decision, a judgment between alternatives. The word has become more and more popular within our culture at large and within business management circles. Often the word "discernment" is used simply as a substitute for "making a decision." But in the Christian tradition, the word is not to be taken so lightly. It involves more than collecting data and deciding according to which choice feels best or conforms to certain predetermined norms. Christian discernment seeks a sense of the presence of God in exploring alternatives. Prayer lies at the heart of Christian discernment.

Discernment in the biblical sense is not choosing between an action that is clearly of God and a direction that is clearly not of God. Rather, it involves choosing the better of two (or more) seemingly godly possibilities. If no such possibilities are available, it involves choosing the lesser of two apparent evils. When discerning a "lesser evil," we are driven to trust that God calls us down that path and that it will work for our good.

Discernment is not for the weakhearted, since it requires wrestling with both angels and demons. A careful process of discernment should be brought to bear when the path to God's will has been obscured, overgrown, or hidden.

One teacher of discernment, Elizabeth Liebert, Professor of Spirituality at San Francisco Theological Seminary, reminds us that the result of discernment is not certainty. Instead of engaging in the risky process of discernment, most of us would rather gaze into a crystal ball that reveals the consequences of our decisions before we make them. But if we were able to look through a crystal ball, there would be no reason for faith. If we could accurately forecast the future, faith would turn to knowledge, and no risk would be involved. But the Christian way is a way of faith, a way of implicit trust in God.

Perhaps it will also help us to acknowledge that objectively perfect discernment does not exist. We can never be sure in advance that we have it right. Only God knows whether or not we are right. The primary purpose of discernment is to make us increasingly available to God over the course of our lives as we deliberately submit our hard choices to God's love. Like other spiritual practices, discernment results in an ever-deepening relationship with Christ and an ever-clearer understanding of who we are before God.

The fruit of our discernment appears most clearly only in retrospect. Those of us who engage in discernment take a long perspective. We realize that recognizing the fruit of discernment occurs over the span of an entire lifetime. As we look back over our lives and the results of the choices we have made, we begin to notice how they have played out. Then we can begin to see patterns, both harmful and helpful, and those patterns give us valuable information for our continuing adventure of discernment.

In part, the accumulation of such information comes with age, which gives perspective on one's life. Say a young man does what seems natural and fulfilling to him in his work. For the most part he thinks nothing of it, but as the years unfold, it becomes obvious to him that he has gifts of imagination and creativity. He draws on these gifts again and again in situations where "newness" is needed and desired. As this man grows older and looks back over his life, he sees clearly that using these gifts has brought him fulfillment. Then he recalls the manner in which these gifts were evoked. Paying attention to the dynamics of these past experiences enables him to recognize situations in which he now finds himself, to use the gifts he has been given, and even to be proactive in responding to certain situations.

Discernment is often spoken of in terms of finding "the will of God" as opposed to following our "human will." For many serious Christians this language is confusing, even destructive. It suggests that God is playing a game with them, that God's will is a fixed, immutable plan, hidden from them until they crack the code. The challenge in this arrangement seems to be to guess the right combination so they can identify the plan.

100

If this were true, only by breaking the code could people become what God intends them to be. Furthermore, this understanding of God's will leads to the assumption that God's way always contradicts what we would normally choose. In fact, some people have taken this misguided notion so far as to say that if they find a certain way unattractive, then it must be God's way.

Ancient Christians were not so limited in their view of God's will. They defined the will of God in more generous and inclusive terms. Words that more accurately express the notion of "God's will" in the discernment tradition are "call" and "invitation." Ron DelBene, who has written extensively about our relationship with God, reminds us that the biblical word translated as "will" comes from both a Hebrew and a Greek word meaning "yearning," the kind of yearning that lovers have for one another.[1]

Discernment is an effort to respond as fully as possible to God's longing for each of us to become "a human being fully alive" (Irenaeus), who is working out "in fear and trembling" the mystery of living fully. Those of us engaging in Christian discernment have generally assumed that our deepest and most powerful desires match God's desires for us. In the process of discernment we seek to uncover our truest and most profound longings, which, we trust, touch God's longings for us. In the place where our yearning meets God's yearning, we begin to experience true rest in God, a sense of profound peace and freedom, and a sacred stillness at the center of our lives. From that place of stillness we can work through the difficulties and challenges that life presents us. And we can revel in the joy we find as we follow God's invitation along the path.

We must continually remind ourselves that discernment has more to do with deepening our relationship with Christ than it does with making right decisions. It is a lifelong process of developing a relationship with God marked by touch-points along the way. No single decision along the way guarantees either "success" or "failure" in our life with Christ. In fact, as Christians we may take many paths to our full expression of human life in Christ. Each decision provides a new opportunity to notice the results of our choices, to attend to how our path matches the way of Christ. And

1. Ron DelBene with Herb Montgomery, *Breath of Life: Discovering Your Breath Prayer* (Minneapolis: Winston Press, 1981), pp. 15-16.

as we make this journey, even our mistakes can prove useful. Nothing is ever wasted! Each time of discernment, whether it has positive or negative results, offers us further practice in hearing and responding to God's invitation. From this perspective, life is a school of discernment in which we study and practice the art every single day.

In general, moments of discernment require judging whether a certain word, action, decision, or conclusion moves us further along God's path than do alternatives. Throughout history, Christians have described this criterion in a variety of ways, each tradition using its own language and images. Some have spoken of discerning between demonic spirits and divine spirits. Others have spoken of choosing between the human spirit and the Holy Spirit. Still others have described judging between the will of God and self-will, as we have already indicated. Whatever language is used, Christian discernment requires judging whether a certain word, action, decision, or conclusion is an appropriate response to God's call at a particular time in our life.

Seeking Discernment: A Story

As leaders, whether or not we have a mature understanding of discernment, we constantly engage in judging and evaluating God's will for us. In spiritually healthy persons, the Spirit seems to work in similar ways. Indeed, from these experiences our spiritual forebears have set forth various ways of discernment. Before exploring some of these more formally defined ways of discernment, we thought it would be instructive to listen to the story of one person seeking to find God's guidance for her life. A faithful church member, she was pursuing one kind of Christian service, but began to feel called to another. Listen to the way she relates her struggle:

> One of the members of the Christian Education Committee at my church suggested that I consider the position of Adult Education Ministries Director. I discounted the notion because I was working on my certificate in Spiritual Formation and did not want to spend my time doing curriculum development and teacher recruitment. I carefully explained to my friends that Christian education was as distinct from spiritual formation as the ABCs are from being fluent

102

in the language. Though I valued and saw the necessity of the ABCs, my calling was in the nurturing of spiritual development in fellow journeyers. My friends smiled at my protests and said, "Yes, I think we've found our next Adult Education Director!"

I wrote in my journal about my perplexity that grew from this conversation. Then two incidents occurred in which other church members asked me to consider applying for the position. Though I initially resisted, their insistence, coupled with my husband's counsel to at least look at the job description, prompted me to accept a copy of the job description. It took me a full day before I was willing to review it. In the intervening time, the Lord clearly asked me, "What if I have brought you, like Esther, to this place at this time to do my work? Are you not even willing to consider the possibility?" I recognized the arrogance of my resistance and began taking a serious look at the position. The tasks seemed demanding. Could I really do the job? Insecurities about my lack of formal training hampered me.

Then I thought: "Our church is very well organized, the basic processes are working well, and I have a good network already established of others already functioning in positions like this one." What really caught my attention was the description given of the desired traits, skills, and experience. They mentioned a deep commitment to the Christian faith, biblical knowledge, a personal lifestyle exemplifying the love of Christ, a desire to lead others to faith in Christ, a zeal and passion for Christian growth with varied personalities, and an understanding of life issues faced by adults. The other items mentioned dealt with organizational and technical skills, all of which I had had experience in developing. A friend of twenty-five years read the job description and said, "Sounds like they wrote this with you in mind. I will be praying for God's will to be done."

My church has always felt like home to me. The first time my husband and I visited it, I met so many wonderful people — who were now the very ones encouraging me to participate in the adult ministry of our church. Each one expressed their conviction that I would be well-suited to this position, and each one kept praying for God's will to be done. I had recently enrolled in the Certificate in Spiritual Formation at Austin Seminary. God amazingly provided the funds for me to go to the certificate program's Immersion Weekend, a three-day introduction to spiritual formation, which propelled me into this area that seemed to be giving definition to my calling.

Could it be that God was indeed calling me to this task?

The process of discerning seems to have been composed of three major elements:

1. placing a priority on daily disciplined presence before God through the reading of Scripture, being still, acknowledging his Godliness and my humanity, offering my intercessions and petitions, and listening in silence for his response through the promptings of Scripture or the Holy Spirit;

2. resisting the inclination to retain a privatized faith by placing myself within a context of Christian counsel for guidance, encouragement, and correction, with a willingness to share openly, listen carefully, and respond prayerfully;

3. trusting the sovereign Holy Spirit to guide and instruct me through the "providential coincidence" of the mundane or unexpected events of the day.

Don't you see in this story reflections of your own efforts to find God's will? As you explore in depth at the more formally articulated, historically developed ways of discernment examined below, note how in embryonic form most of them are represented in this layperson's story.

Models of Discernment

In the Christian tradition, the work of discernment has always included at least five elements. These elements have been explored in so many places and by so many competent writers that we believe it is unnecessary to examine them in depth again.[2] Still, a brief overview of these elements will help set the stage for a further consideration of the art of discernment.

First, discernment has always been grounded in studying, praying

---

2. Ben Campbell Johnson, *Discerning God's Will* (Decatur, Ga.: CTS Press, 1999). Dallas Willard, *In Search of Guidance: Developing a Conversational Relationship with God* (Grand Rapids: Zondervan Publishing House, 1993).

with, and interpreting the Old and New Testaments. Although these Scriptures contain an unfolding revelation of God, it is not difficult to see the direction in which they are pointing. For Christians the standard for discernment is always Jesus Christ. Our choices should express him.

Second, the wisdom of past Christians informs our discernment. The steadfast commitment of St. Polycarp when he was asked to deny Christ gives us a model for courage. He could not deny his Lord. In the same way, the "I have a dream" speech by Martin Luther King Jr. helps us see what devout followers of Christ have said and done. These believers inspire and direct us with their insight and courage.

But we need not reach far back into Christian history to get help with discernment — a point that brings us to the third element: seeking help from a brother or sister with whom we worship or pray. When we share our dilemma and our options with them, they often advise us with great wisdom. They share their own experiences with us, and God speaks through them to confirm or refine our discernment.

Fourth, not only do we look to others for guidance, but we also listen to the movement of God within our own souls. For a long time the people of faith have discerned the leading of God from a sense of peace, a depth of conviction, or an inner knowing. We should not interpret these movements within in isolation from all the other modes of discernment, but they help confirm our knowledge of God's ways of self-revelation.

Fifth and finally, our discernment is helped through our experience of the culture in which we live. There are times when the light of God shines through the discoveries, insights, and wisdom of our culture. For this reason, when we seek to discern God's guidance in ethical matters, we should familiarize ourselves with all the facts relative to an issue.

Perhaps an illustration will help us see the interplay of the elements of discernment more clearly. Suppose a doctor is treating a patient with a terminal illness. The patient is on life support in the hospital, and it appears that the patient has no hope of getting well. How does the doctor decide whether or not to take this person off life support?

When the faithful doctor looks at Scripture, he finds instructive words like "You shall not kill." Would taking away the life support of this person amount to killing in the biblical sense? What about the text that says, "Love your neighbor as yourself"? Would the doctor want to continue to exist with no hope of resuming a quality life? Would the patient?

In addition to consulting the texts and the witness of those who have gone before him, the doctor will certainly talk with the patient's family. In seeking their wisdom, he will pray for guidance and invite their prayers. If at this point the doctor reaches the preliminary conclusion that the patient should be taken off life support, he may experience internal conflict because, as a physician, he has taken an oath to save life, not destroy it. How does he keep this commitment when all the indicators say the patient should be permitted to die?

Besides weighing all the relevant commentary from the Christian tradition, the medical tradition, and the patient's family, the doctor listens to his contemporaries. What do they say about the meaning of health, the meaning of dying, and the preservation of life at all costs? This struggling, faithful person may receive help from insights in contemporary literature.

This real-life situation makes it remarkably clear that there are no easy answers. Discernment does not always produce a clear direction. Nevertheless, armed with insights from Scripture and other significant texts, the witness of others, our own sense of peace and conviction, and what we learn from current cultural sources (which may not be religious in nature), we can find the courage to act in faith.

Along with these traditional ways of discerning the yearning of God for us, we find more refined ways of discernment suggested by St. Ignatius, the Quaker tradition, and the practice of group discernment. While these first two forms of discernment have much in common with the general elements of discernment, they also contain particular emphases and approaches that make them unique.

Ignatian Discernment

In the sixteenth century, Ignatius of Loyola wrote his *Spiritual Exercises* to help committed Christians turn their lives more fully toward God and find their calling. Christianity has produced no more complete a description of discernment than the Ignatian *Exercises*. For over four hundred years, either implicitly or explicitly, this model has been the dominant form of discernment in the West. While it is not our intent to offer here a full description of the Ignatian process of discernment, we can offer an overview that we believe will assist you in your discernment.

106

The *Exercises* are a prayerful discernment process that covers four movements — Ignatius called them "weeks" — in spiritual formation. They move from examining yourself in relation to God, to praying through the life and ministry of Jesus, to praying yourself into Jesus' experience of the crucifixion, and, finally, to praying your way into the resurrection. This model of discernment can be undertaken as a thirty-day retreat, an eight-day retreat, or a retreat in your daily life.

According to Ignatius, faithful discernment requires certain characteristics. Drawing on the work of Elizabeth Liebert, we can define these characteristics as a desire to discern, a knowledge of self, humility, courage, a commitment to put God first, and a willingness to follow God's guidance. We will examine each of these important aspects of discernment and raise questions that may be helpful to you in exploring discernment issues. We will then outline the basic steps in the process of discernment. We strongly recommend that you identify an issue about which you need discernment and then apply each of these steps to it. First, let's look at the characteristics:

A desire to discern: In prayer and in all aspects of the spiritual life, desire forms the foundation of our movement toward God. We must deeply desire to discern God's call — and be aware of that desire. As you examine your issue, ask yourself this question: Do you truly desire to know the will of God, the direction that will ultimately be best for you?

A knowledge of self: This knowledge primarily involves the ability to notice and explore a wide range of movements within our being. What are we feeling, imagining, thinking, sensing, willing, and intending for our life? What do these movements connect to in your life? Given what you know about yourself, what aspects of your personhood do you think are likely to get in the way of your hearing the yearning of God? How can you minimize your vulnerable points to more clearly see the intention of God?

Humility: In this context, "humility" refers to an openness to receive the input of others and the recognition that God does not seek to diminish us but always exceeds us. This kind of humility assumes that we are not the fount of all wisdom and that much wisdom comes from beyond us. Can you acknowledge that you do not have all the answers to your issue? Can you believe that there is One outside of you and beyond you who can lead you into the answer to your deepest questions?

Courage: We can make no move in God's direction if we are frozen in insecurity or stuck in uncertainty. The process of discernment demands that we be bold enough to trust again and again that God has faith in us. We need courage just to come into the presence of God, but it takes additional courage to take steps toward a future that we see only dimly. What fears do you have that could prevent you from hearing God's word to you?

A commitment to put God first: To truly put God first, we need to be "indifferent" to the things and concerns of the world. We need to "seek first the reign of God and God's righteousness," and from that place we can begin to choose our path. Put God first and embrace the things of the world from God's perspective. By "indifference" we do not mean passive uncaring but an openness to whatever God may say. In seeking discernment, can you let yourself be indifferent to the path God chooses for you? If you lack indifference, you may secretly hope that God's intention for you follows a particular course. This secret desire creates static that can prevent you from clearly hearing the voice of God.

A willingness to follow God's guidance: No matter how clearly we discern God's call, our discernment will mean nothing if we do not have a strong willingness to follow the way we discover. It is in following that our discernment comes alive. When we see the course that God is revealing, we may very well feel an initial reluctance that confuses our desire to follow. If we should respond this way, we can always pray that God will give us the will to desire the way being revealed. And we may need to ask God to be patient with us while we are getting our human desire in line with the divine desire.

With these characteristics, we can undertake a process of discernment that will carry us onto a fruitful path with Christ. Again, Elizabeth Liebert points us toward the steps involved in this process:

1. Formulate as clearly and specifically as possible the question to which you want to discern an answer: "Shall I do A or B?" For example, ask "Shall I move to Salem or stay in Columbus?" not "Shall I move?" Even in the process of clarifying the question, you begin to discern its answer. So spend time in conversation with God about the exact nature of your question.

2. Pray to be turned toward God rather than focused on the transient things of earth. Also ask others to pray for you. Keep praying this prayer until you sense your desire turning more fully to the desire of God.

3. Gather data about your question. This dimension takes advantage

of your practical skills as an intelligent, capable, curious child of God. What issues are raised around the question? Whom does it affect and how? What does Scripture have to say concerning your question? What does the Christian community of both the past and the present say? What have you learned in your life that addresses this question? What do other people and the culture around you say? Maybe you can draw on management skills to list and analyze what you have discovered. Record the pros and cons of your potential choices.

4. Pray through the pros and cons of your issue. Here the process of discernment goes beyond standard ways of analyzing data. Your prayer should focus on how each of the pros and cons struck you, given all the information you have gathered. As you bring these positives and negatives before God in prayer, pay attention to how you feel about each of them — uneasy, angry, full of distaste, apathetic, fearful, happy, or at peace.

As part of this process, use your imagination to pray about the issue. With all the information you have, imagine that you are in Jesus' presence, listening to him speak with you about the issue. Also, imagine you are advising someone else on the same issue. What would you say to them? If you were going to die in a few months, how would you feel about this issue? Finally, engage Jesus in a written dialogue in which you ask him a question, write down what you "hear" his answer to be, and then respond to that answer. Continue this process until you have a half-dozen interchanges with him.

5. Make the decision that seems best. At this stage of discernment, the choice has often become obvious. If it has not, have the courage to make the decision that has the most evidence, both internal and external, in its favor.

6. Bring the decision back to prayer. Pray again as you did before, but this time from the perspective of having made the decision. In this way you begin to "live" into the decision, discovering how it fits with your life in Christ.

7. Live with your decision before acting on it. If your circumstances will permit, live your life for a number of days or weeks as if you have made the decision but without acting on it. Something happens inside us when we live with a tentative decision as if it were our final decision. Our feelings may embrace the decision as the right one, or they may create in us unrest and a lack of peace, signaling us to reconsider our choice. Dur-

ing this period of "living into" the decision, tell people you trust about your decision and gather their responses. Once again, bring your decision before God in prayer in the way we have suggested.

8. Look for inner peace and freedom. Throughout all of these steps, pay attention to your sense of inner peace and freedom, a sense of stillness before God — even when the consequences of your decision seem difficult or trying or impossible to carry out. Subtle and elusive as it is, this deep, expansive sense of peace-filled freedom is an important indication that you are close to the place where your most profound yearning meets God's longing for you. It may be quite helpful to meet with a mature spiritual friend whose guidance can help you notice when and how deeply you experience this sense of freedom and stillness before God.

9. Follow and learn. The disciples followed Jesus and were taught about their lives with God. Likewise, after we act upon our decision, we must pay prayerful attention to its consequences in our lives. When you have begun to follow the guidance you received, notice the fruit in your life. What are you learning about your life with God? What are you discovering that will serve you well when the next time of discernment comes? Are you experiencing the gifts of the Spirit blossoming more fully in your life?

Although we have given a certain order to the basic steps in the process of discernment, you should not think of these in a mechanistic way; they are principles. You will discover that the movement through the process does not always occur as we have outlined it. In all likelihood there will be times when you have begun the process and have received your answer before you reach the final steps. Clearly it is important to remember that keeping attuned to God throughout the discernment process is essential.

Quaker Discernment

The Quaker tradition also has gifted Christianity with a helpful model for discernment. In the Quaker model, a group of people gathers to help an individual with the discernment process. This model depends on a group of five to eight trusted persons who will follow the process with genuine understanding and the proper sensibility. This may be a group that is already practiced in the art of discernment; if not, they can be easily trained. This group is called a "Clearness Committee" because its role is to help the person seeking discernment understand more clearly his or her particular issue, hear more accurately God's call, and see more clearly the path God is inviting him or her to take.

When a person begins to realize the desire for discernment around a particular issue, she notifies each member of the group and arranges a time to meet for discernment. Before the meeting, she writes three to five pages in which she clearly and concretely defines the issue around which she seeks discernment. In this written definition she should name the issue and describe its significance, its history, and the circumstances that surround it. She should also describe all the influences in her present situation that may have a bearing on her discernment — Scripture, the teachings and practice of the Christian community (past and present), the surrounding culture, the natural world, other people's lives, and her own personhood. Several days before the meeting, she gives a copy of her writing to each of the members.

In preparation, the committee members will pray about what has been offered to them. They will prepare themselves for the time they will spend in the meeting.

The meeting itself follows a simple format. We will describe it as though you, the reader, are the person seeking discernment.

When the hour has come, welcome everyone who has come to the meeting. Thank them for their willingness to participate in the process. Ask for a volunteer to be the secretary; he or she will record the flow of the conversation for your future reference. Ask for another volunteer to be the facilitator. This person will keep the process on track, making sure it retains the proper pace and focus. Then invite the group to enter into an extended time of silence.

When you are ready, break the silence and state the discernment issue as you understand it. For example, "I would like help in discerning between beginning a course of training in pastoral counseling or a course in spiritual direction." You should also outline any new developments that have arisen since you wrote your description of the issue.

At this point, the group members may begin to ask questions. Members of the committee should be clear that their only role is to ask questions. They should be cautioned against asking questions that contain implicit advice: "Don't you think that you should consider your mother in

111

this decision?" The question, of course, implies that "yes" is the correct answer. If the woman's mother is important in the discernment, the question would be better stated this way: "How does this decision affect your mother?" No one person should dominate the questioning. And the pace of the questions should be slow, with ample pauses between each question.

After a question is asked, the group becomes silent, letting you, the seeker, reflect on the question. Remember that you are not compelled to answer any of the questions. You have several choices: You may respond to the questions as they are posed, or you may choose not to respond to some or any of the questions, or you may mentally file them away for further consideration.

End the session after one hour — or earlier if you feel the meeting has achieved your goal. Prayers for guidance and courage may be offered at the end of the meeting.

Many persons have found this approach very helpful in their process of discernment. Its use of silence, thoughtful questions, and prayer make it a powerful model.

The Practice of Group Discernment

The two models of discernment we have described are intended especially for individuals. While individual discernment is important, many issues in a congregation's life also cry out for communal discernment. Congregations and groups within congregations desire and need to discover more fully God's invitations to them. Unfortunately, the discernment tradition has not developed clear models for group discernment. Recently, however, models have begun to take shape, pointing the way to a fruitful future for group discernment. Because these emerging models tend to be rather complex, lengthy, subtle, or require a particular kind of trained leadership, many congregational groups may not be able to engage them. The contemporary church still awaits a clear and practicable form of discernment for groups.

This is not the place to develop a full model for group discernment, but we do want to offer one example of how congregational groups like committees and boards can begin to develop the sensibilities and skills necessary for discernment. One rather simple process is based on the *Lectio Divina* tradition. It follows the format of group *Lectio Divina.*

This process assumes that all involved share the characteristics vital for discernment that we mentioned earlier: a desire to discern, self-knowledge, humility, courage, a commitment to put God first, and the willingness to follow God's guidance. In addition, group discernment rests on the conviction that God's wisdom comes most fully through a group and depends on members' willingness to trust the wisdom of the group.

Group discernment cannot work if we come to decision-making groups with our own agendas, ready to lobby for our own ideas and advocate for our own values. If we bring this fixed attitude, we will simply argue on behalf of our own agendas and try to persuade others to join our side. Group discernment looks not for a majority vote but for clarity about what God desires us to be and do.

Self-centered attitudes destroy group discernment. Members of the group must come with only one agenda: to listen for God through the collective wisdom of the group. Instead of believing that he or she has the complete answer, each member comes to the group trusting that he or she brings some tiny piece of wisdom that will be valuable in the process. Only by putting all the group's pieces of wisdom together will true wisdom emerge, a whole greater than the sum of its parts. Each member looks for the direction of the Spirit and waits for a sense of heartfelt unanimity.

It will be helpful for us to think of spiritual wisdom as residing in God's Well, a receptacle of infinite supply. The gathered group is like the well that contains the pool of divine wisdom. Each group member comes to this well with two water containers. One is a tiny vial containing the droplets of the individual's wisdom. The other is a large bucket, open and empty. The members pour into the well the water droplets from their vials. When those droplets flow together, the pool of wisdom grows and changes. The group can look into the pool that is formed and describe for one another what wisdom they see there. And they can fill their buckets full of that wisdom.

Many groups may not be ready for group discernment. The group members may need to develop experience in the practices of individual spiritual formation or discernment before joining together in the group

113

exercise. But assuming a group is ready, how might it try to move together toward discernment of God's call? We offer the following example.

Suppose that in the process of creating a yearly budget, a Mission Committee realizes that, because of limited funds, they must choose between two mission projects outside the congregation's life. How might they as a group move forward in discernment? Here is one way that discernment can be approached:

1. Set a meeting time, state the issue, and ask the committee members to prepare by praying for discernment and for a sense of God's presence.

2. As part of the preparation, ask one or two people to gather information on the two mission projects. Tell them that no more than one page should be devoted to each project. Have them use these questions in gathering data and writing the report: What is the project's purpose? Who organizes and administers it? How much funding is required? Exactly what will the funding provide? What need does it address? How will the committee or congregation be involved (beyond funding)? Remind them to search for validation that each project is faithful to God's call. When the reports are completed, send copies of them to the committee members. Ask them to read through the reports before the meeting, imagining as they do so that they are seeking a way to represent Jesus to the world through the mission.

3. When the committee gathers for the meeting, the following agenda will help guide the process:

- Describe the steps the group will follow.
- Begin with a prayer asking for God's presence and wisdom.
- Ask the members to settle into stillness, close their eyes, and begin to let their minds consider the significant aspects of the congregation's life. Have a facilitator slowly read the following phrases: "Sunday morning worship . . . our weekend retreat . . . the mission trip to Mexico . . . the men's group . . . The October potluck. . . ." After the reading of each phrase, invite the committee members to notice what word or picture comes to them when this aspect of the congregation is mentioned. Ask them to share their word or picture/image, one at a time, until everyone has spoken who wishes to. Encourage them not to rush. Phrase by phrase, review each part of the congregation's life.

- Continue in the same spirit of attentiveness. Slowly read — twice — the section from the report on the first project that describes how it is faithful to God's call. Before the reading, invite the group to listen and pay close attention to their sense of whether or not this connects with the congregation. After a period of silence, invite everyone to share their reflections, with no "crosstalk" or comments after each person shares. (If a group wishes, they could express their reflections through prose, poetry, or some form of art — perhaps drawing — before speaking.)
- Reflect on the second project in the same fashion.
- Offer a prayer of thanks for the congregation and the two projects.
- Conduct a general discussion of these questions: What have we learned about our connection to these projects? About the congregation's connection? What is our sense now of which project God is inviting us to embrace?

Perhaps the group will have come to a sense of unanimity at this point. If not, the members may want to take a break, gather again for a time of extended silence, and then share any new reflections on the issues. This may lead to a sense of unanimity or to a sense that the topic needs further attention.

As we noted earlier, not every group is capable of engaging fruitfully in the discernment process. In working with congregations, however, we have found that an ability to engage in group discernment tends to come naturally if a group's members are individually practicing traditional exercises of spiritual formation. Over time, individuals who are engaged in these practices begin to develop a communal trust, a deeper sense of God's ways, and an ability to discern God's call. Group discernment can then proceed without the antagonism that often develops in group decision-making. The sense of trust and community develops slowly, but we believe it is ultimately more fruitful to wait for this to happen than to impose a process on a group that doesn't match its skills and sensibilities.

Having said that, we still believe it is possible to gradually introduce a group to the process of communal discernment. Inviting a group to explore their decision-making through the discernment tradition helps them begin to develop new capacities for sensing God's call, even if the group fails in their initial efforts in discernment of particular issues. The important thing is to begin introducing a group to new ways of approaching decision-making. Invite them to try "experiments," like some of the practices we have described. Help them feel secure and confident to report how this experiment worked for them. You may work with this process in an open-ended fashion by eliminating the need to come to a decision. Help the group experience a more prayerful, less analytical, less agenda-laden approach to an issue. Later, this experience can be part of the data they use to reach a decision.

No matter what form of discernment you practice, whether individually or communally, this discipline is essential in the deepening of the spiritual nature of the church. As we notice again and again how God has been with us and is with us, we discover more clearly our direction with God. It is as if each discerning movement plants a seed on our life's journey. When we review our various encounters with God, we can see what has grown from these seeds. Some have fallen on rocky ground, some on hard paths. Weeds have choked some; others have been scorched. But a good number have taken root and are flourishing. They were planted in God's intended places. As we keep looking back and examining them, we notice that they eventually begin to form a pattern. And with that pattern in mind, we can more clearly see the shape of the path that will take us most directly to God's intention for our lives.

We are so accustomed to treating decisions solely as sources of anxiety, tension, and division. Too often we invest our very beings in a decision; we attach our sense of self-worth to how the decision turns out. A win/lose view of decisions keeps us in a bind. When, for example, the group does not make the decision we favor, we lose not only the thrill of victory but also our sense of dignity.

But the long tradition of discernment reminds us that there is more to life with God than "correct" decisions. There is forgiveness. There is growth. Whether or not you make the "right" decision, it can never be perfect, and God extends forgiving grace to us again and again. God is the God of second chances. This second chance comes because God has such a powerful, endless longing to be intimate with us. After all, the point is not to get it right but to let each chance for discernment be another opportunity to open ourselves more fully to God and to discover more clearly how God is with us. In the very process of discerning we enter more fully into a sense of divine intimacy.

QUESTIONS FOR REFLECTION AND DISCUSSION

1. What are the general principles of discernment? How do you evaluate them?
2. How would you compare the Ignatian model with the Quaker model?
3. Name a discernment issue facing your church. See what happens when you apply the general principles to this issue.
4. Where do you personally need discernment? Which of the approaches seems best for your need? Why?

SUGGESTIONS FOR JOURNALING

1. In a few sentences, describe the major issue in your life that calls for discernment.
2. Apply each of the appropriate principles derived from Liebert's list. As you write down the applications, new insights will surprise you.
3. Where do you feel stuck or afraid? Compose prayers about these blocks.
4. Write a prayer stating your indifference (whatever God sees as best for you) and commit the issue to God.

Chapter Eight

REFRESHMENT FOR THE SOUL

Pilgrims who go to present-day Nazareth discover, in the heart of the city, a well. This ancient well dates back before the days of Jesus. Over the centuries, the destruction of settlements, debris, windblown dust, the refuse of human consumption, and the residue of paving materials have conspired to raise the streets and pathways around the well. Perhaps the site would have been lost long ago if a group of faithful believers had not built a small, unpretentious building, a sanctuary, over the well to preserve it. Christians today still visit the well to find refreshment for body and soul.

To get to the well, you must find your way along busy thoroughfares, wade through the crowds, and descend several steps to enter the cool darkness of the sanctuary. Once inside, you will find the well tucked away in a sort of alcove. If you wish, you can lower a tiny metal pail down the small, rock-lined shaft and draw water from a pool many feet below. With a dipper used by many, you may taste the refreshing water that bubbles up from unseen depths.

You will hear your guide describe how important this well has been in the life of the city of Nazareth. It has served the people of this city since the town was established many centuries ago. During Jesus' childhood, it was the town's only source of water, fed then, as now, by deep, underground springs. Women and children gathered there daily to draw water for drinking and cooking. Surely Jesus came to this well, drew water from it, and drank.

Perhaps this very well provided the original experience Jesus had with water from a well. Could it have been this experience that shaped his conversation years later with a Samaritan woman? This ancient well in Naza-reth speaks metaphorically of another kind of Well. It reminds us first of all of the importance of water for life, health, cleanliness, and survival. But the setting of this well also hints at the numerous ways that debris conceals the source of life as time passes. Small wonder that the well has always been a metaphor for God, since it easily speaks of the divine depth, the accessible, mysterious source of life, and the fount of "living water."

How remarkable that we may drink from the same well Jesus drank from. We can drink from a well in Nazareth, but — even more astound-ing — we can also draw from the same inner Well that Jesus drew from. For this Well exists in every person. In every leader in Christ's church there is an inner depth that opens to God, and this depth offers us the possibility of descending into our being and meeting God.

But the setting of the well in Nazareth hints at the numerous ways in which debris can conceal the source of life as time passes. And we may find that this is exactly what has happened to our pathway to the Well — that it has become layered with the dust and debris of apathy, paved over by human effort, choked by weeds of anger, and littered with the garbage of shame and fear. All these obstacles make the path to the Well difficult to travel. And through disuse the path becomes more and more difficult to discern. But today leaders of the church must find the Well, must drink from the Well. It is a matter of life and death for them and the church!

Signs of Thirst

No matter how deeply dedicated we as leaders may be, after months or years of service, our energy often runs low. Dreams that burned with the fire of imagination begin to grow dimmer as time passes; passion for the work of God cools after months or years of intensive labor; and the vivid sense of a high calling becomes dull when we feel consumed by our re-sponsibilities. These dulling experiences of ministry in the church suggest to us that we need a renewal of the life of the Spirit.

The wear and tear of ministry on both lay leaders and clergy calls for a return to the source of our dreams and passion and call. Those who do not find their way to the Well for this refreshment begin to experience a

119

rash of painful symptoms. Perhaps you have experienced these symptoms or have seen them in others:

- losing passion for God
- struggling weekly to spend time with God
- lacking energy in work and service
- feeling controlled by a divisive spirit
- feeling a sense of drudgery when facing simple tasks
- dreading the morning and the day's work ahead
- wondering about who God is and how God works
- sensing the Presence far away
- questioning one's call and vocation
- avoiding intimacy with God or even conversations about God

All Christian leaders from time to time find these telltale symptoms cropping up in their lives. Some experience these feelings as temptations and resist them with the shield of faith. Others mistakenly believe that these symptoms make them shallow and worthless in the work of Christ. But these experiences do not need to be received as temptations or as signs of unfaithfulness. Instead, they may be understood as wake-up calls announcing a new, revolutionary way ahead. Leaders in the Church of Jesus Christ should not expect to participate in a spiritual revolution without encountering serious struggle. In these times of testing, it is important for leaders to uncover the source of their symptoms and find ways to transform the practices and attitudes that sap the spirit out of them.

Even if you find these symptoms multiplying in your life, there is hope. Remember that when Elijah was sitting under the broom tree in the wilderness, he wanted to die. To save his life, he was running from the murderous Jezebel, and yet under the broom tree he prayed to die. (What a contradiction — being afraid to die, yet wanting to die.) The angel of the Lord appeared, twice offering him bread and water, and from it he received the strength to journey to Horeb, the mount of God. Through his cry for help and the response from the messenger of God, Elijah received the necessary energy to set out on the path to Horeb. Finding strength for the journey into the wilderness began with his thirst for God.

For Elijah and for us, the path to the Well begins with this thirsty longing, this deep desire for the Spirit. This desire for intimacy with God comes to us in many different forms. It may appear as an emptiness that yearns for fulfillment and then suddenly turns into self-criticism for a lack of interest or commitment.

Or, this desire may manifest itself in a dryness of spirit when we are preparing to teach a lesson. On other days, we remember, the words came easily to our lips, we may have felt inspired as we spoke, and our words seemed to penetrate the hearts of our hearers. Afterward, members of the class spoke, indicating not only their appreciation but also the resolves they had made as a result of the truth taught. When these results are not forthcoming, and every teaching task requires more and more effort, maybe we are being beckoned to the Well.

This same feeling of flatness in life and work may express itself as boredom when we lead a committee into its work. Committee work can be exciting and exhilarating when we have a sense of the presence of Christ in the midst of the group, when ideas flow freely, when members of the group hear the call of Christ to participate in the mission. Isn't it strange how this same stimulating committee can become dull in its imagination and boring in its discussion of needs or programs? The loss of the sense of Presence may be yet another way in which the Lord calls us back to the Well.

This feeling of flatness may also permeate a short-term mission trip, a trip that in the past has always been a deep source of inspiration but now fails to nourish either the group or us. When the group set out to help a village of poor people build a church, they had such high expectations that they would receive more than they gave, and that the restless spirit within them would be healed. But that didn't happen. Something went wrong. The group missed the renewing effect of ministry. Or perhaps they didn't notice what God was doing during this venture?

Too often we not only do the work of God for our own inspiration, but we decide how God manifests Godself to us. When God does not appear in the ways we have expected, we judge that God was not present. Our expectations rob us of encountering the God who is present and active in our midst because we do not seek God as God is. This is another indication that we need to find our way back to the Well, the source of our inspiration and discernment.

Perhaps our need to return to the Well manifests itself in first one and then another of these symptoms. A conscious thirst, a feeling of emptiness, a flatness of spirit, a disappointment with results — these inner signals are invitations to the Well.

Maybe this simple exercise will help you to identify your invitation to the refreshing waters of the Spirit. Settle yourself away from distractions. Ask God to be with you in this time. Allow yourself to focus on a question Jesus once asked a blind man: "What do you want me to do for you?" Ruminate on this question, repeating it again and again to yourself.

Imagine Jesus directing the question to you. Let it continue to resonate within you until it has evoked all your yearnings for this moment in time. Allow Jesus' answer to form in you, first as feelings, then as images, and then as words. Pay special attention to all the communications of Christ to you as you make your way to the Well.

Whatever your leadership role in the Church of Jesus Christ, there is a cup for you at the Well. Take time to rake away the debris from the pathway and find the Well. At the Well you will receive what you need for the journey ahead of you.

At the Well

Numerous pathways, though overgrown and strewn with rubble, lead to the Well. Some seekers of the path have found "stillness" to be the most direct way to the Well. "Be still and know that I am God."

Others have found the pathway of "remembering" to be most direct for them. Again and again the psalmist says, "But then I remember . . ." Memory helps us revisit other times and places when our spirits reveled in a profound sense of God's Presence.

Sometimes we awake to the fact that we are at the Well through no effort of our own. Our thirst has been the pathway that brought us to the Well, or the awareness of the invitation seemingly drew us directly without our discipline.

All of these pathways lead to the Well. Some are more direct, some easier to traverse. And some pathways seem to be for one time in the journey, some for another. When our lives are dry and parched, the important thing for us is getting to the Well. The Well is the dimension of depth, the habitation of the Holy, the place of meeting between the human spirit and the Holy Spirit. How can mortals not be awakened and renewed in spirit when they come before God? But how can they speak meaningfully of such an experience?

Words fail, all images become inadequate, and the human imagination staggers in the presence of the Holy. Most of the great spiritual writers claim that no words can describe the human encounter with the holy, yet this does not stop them from writing volume upon volume about the indescribable. Encountering our God results in an outpouring of life that cannot be contained.

We too are attempting the impossible in this book: to speak of the indescribable moment of being in the presence of the Holy One. We too will make an effort to say what cannot be said. What is it like to be here at the Well before God?

At the Sacred Well we receive a sense of being before the Ultimately Real, being before God. In the presence of the Creator, our attachments to earthly success and to earth's fading praise melt away. In these moments we know that only God's glory and majesty matter. Our view of life changes dramatically when our earthly frame glimpses the holiness of God.

Being in the sacred space offers rest — rest from our labor, rest from all striving, rest from inner and outer conflicts, rest from agendas, and rest from the desire for recognition. In this book we have advocated a rest in God that leaves results in God's hands and freedom in our spirits. At the Well we find the strength to let go, and our emphasis strangely shifts from "doing" to "being." In this sacred dimension our lives are measured by their capacity to appreciate being, to let things be, and to worship the One who Is (Exod. 3:14).

In the Sacred Depth of the Soul we discover a sense of being and letting be. In so much of our conscious life, we are driven, obsessive-compulsive leaders who feel that we must change something or be changed by some action. In God there is an amazing sense of letting be! Even our work on a committee or our visit to a fellow church member can be yielded up to God, whether or not it seemed successful.

Lingering in the deep Well of the soul permits an unconscious, nondirected transformation to take place. In this inner sanctuary we do not pray and struggle with ourselves, but we are changed nevertheless. As certainly as rainy nights turn into sunny days and the caterpillar turns into a beautiful butterfly, we also change. By simply resting in the cocoon of grace, we are transformed by the Spirit of God.

At the Well, we receive vision. The intuition about the way into the future arises from the Well! We do not know the way; it must be given to us. Perhaps you discovered this when you were searching for a vision for your life or for that of the congregation. Of course, no matter how clearly this vision appears in your mind, over a period of time it tends to fade. The circumstances of life batter it or challenge it, and it requires all your efforts to follow the dream. But when you visit the Well, the same God who gave you the vision renews it with strong assurance.

Don't these enticements draw you once again to the Well, where you may drink of the water that quenches your thirst? We strongly suggest that spiritual leaders, both clergy and lay, make frequent personal and communal trips to the Well. Unless we return and become refreshed, all the telltale symptoms of burnout will appear in our lives, and ministry will lose its luster.

Water from the Well

Practical-minded persons wonder what comes to us from the Well. What is the consequence of drinking from the Well? How does it affect our lives and leadership?

Drinking water from the Well gives us a sense of connectedness with God. Often the connection lies beyond our capacity to describe or name, but the sense of being in communion carries its own reality; it is a knowing "beyond knowing."

The kind of spiritual leadership that we dream of depends upon this connection. At its core, spiritual leadership consists of relating to God everything we do in the ministry of the church (and in life, for that matter). We worship to glorify God; we teach to inform persons about God; we preach God's Word to evoke a dialogue with God; we visit, serve, and give out of a sense of our union with God's purposes. If we lose our sense of connectedness with God, our efforts become empty human gestures devoid of meaning.

Water from the Well gives preachers a conviction about the message they preach, and it gives assurance to lay leaders too. Everyone leaves the

124

Well with a deeper conviction about the Divine. We believe this new certitude is a gift of grace; it is not self-imposed or self-generated but gratuitously given by God to those who come to the Well for a drink.

In a mysterious way this conviction of God flows into the creation of a sermon, infuses the delivery, and communicates a power beyond that of the preacher. And people in the pew recognize an indescribable difference in both the preacher and the Word preached.

Water from the Well gives us a clearer sense of who we are and what our life is about. This clarity touches not only our work in the church but the whole of our lives. Even if we do not feel fragmented and burned out, water from this Well deepens the truth of God in us. If we neglect the water from this spiritual Well, we will become diffused in vision, fragmented in life, and frustrated in our work. Water from the Well cleanses, clarifies, and restores.

Water from the Well gives us the courage to go on with ministry in the face of self-doubt, criticism, and seeming failure. Ministry in the church today is both challenging and frustrating to clergy and laity alike. The church today stands between the times, with one group clinging to the past and the other group clamoring for change. Those of us who don't take one side or the other find ourselves caught in the middle, and the tension steadily wears our spirits down. Being with God imparts the courage to move forward in the face of opposition, to persist in times of temptation, and to take risk when much is at stake.

Finding a Pathway to the Well

We have described many of the pathways to the Well, those various spiritual practices that help us journey toward a deeper intimacy with Christ. But sometimes the first step on the journey seems daunting. Perhaps you long to drink from the Well, but something stops you — an interior block, a hesitation, a fear, or simple inertia.

Common wisdom tells us that it is best to start small. If you begin an exercise program, begin with simple practices. Muscles need a gentle introduction to the hard work ahead. Eventually you may be able to lift two hundred pounds or run ten miles. But if you begin with the big lift or the long run, your body will rebel, your muscles will be strained, your grand aspirations will be shattered — and, furthermore, you will have an excuse not to proceed!

The same wisdom applies to the spiritual life. If you choose a pathway to the Well that is too steep or too rugged for you, you will find weariness, not refreshment, for your soul. Some may travel strenuous pathways, but it is unwise for you to follow their path. Perhaps you think of them as holy persons, but attaining "holiness" is not the point of the journey. Their longing for holiness may be nothing more than a temptation to self-glorification. Remember that the deepest desire placed in our hearts is for God alone. The desire for holiness can masquerade as desire for God — but it can never replace the yearning for Godself. So, instead of overextending yourself on the spiritual path, consider how you might take the smallest of steps toward the Well.

An Example

Perhaps a description of one woman's search for a way to the Well will give you some ideas. Pat, a single mother of two teenagers, serves as an elder in her church. As a businesswoman and a homemaker, she was having difficulty finding the time and energy for the practices that would nourish her spiritual journey. Recognizing her longing for God, she went to a spiritual director, seeking a way to refresh her soul.

In her first meeting with the spiritual friend, Pat nervously confessed that she had difficulty praying. "When I sit down to focus on God, nothing happens," she said. "All I do is think of other things — the things on my to-do list, the money problems with my business, my children's problems in school — that kind of stuff. And that's not the hardest part. Really, the toughest part is just doing it, just taking time to pray. Quite honestly, I don't really like it at all. Praying, that is."

The guide asked her to describe her prayer time, and Pat continued: "Well, I try to pray early in the morning, before the kids get up. I sit at my kitchen table. I get a candle and the Bible, and I sit down and try to focus on God, really try to focus. I say to myself, 'Okay, here I am, ready to pray and focus on a Scripture passage and on you, God.' I know this is what I should be doing, but it seems so heavy, so burdensome. And I find myself not wanting to be there. The room is cold, the chair is hard, and

I'm sleepy. I don't feel any freedom of the Spirit. Praying doesn't seem inviting at all. I keep thinking that I'll feel invited, you know? I keep thinking that Christ will invite me to commune with him. But nothing like that happens during my prayer time."

Pat's patient listener asked her to step back from her prayer time and to explore the flow of her day. As she reflected on a typical day, she noted that it included an early-morning rush to help her children get ready for school, followed by the bustle of business activity at the office all day. She moved at an exhausting pace. "The routine doesn't slow until evening," Pat explained, "but then I do quiet down."

Then she drew a very detailed picture of the evening's respite: "I sit in the darkness of my bedroom, cradled in a stack of pillows on my bed. I light a few candles, put on soft music, and then my mind wanders over the day. I consider what happened to me, how I responded to people at work, how I feel about decisions I've made, and generally how I lived my life this day. Sometimes I write thoughts in my journal as ideas come to me from my reflections. I like to underscore lessons I've learned, and note how I can become a better person. It's my most creative time. Amazing insights come to me that help me sort out issues in my life.

"Occasionally the children come into my bedroom, and we talk about their day. They tell me about their faith struggles, their problems at school or with friends. And I tell them how things are with me. It's nice, really nice. This time of day feels very soft and warm and inviting. In that setting I feel loved, and I feel loving. Every day I look forward to this evening time. I can't wait for it."

Do you see how Pat finds her way to the Well? She had been laboring under the assumption that the path to the Well consisted of sitting on a cold, hard chair and forcing herself to focus on God and a Scripture passage. What if her path to the Well consisted of a quiet room, soft music, burning candles, and relaxation on a stack of pillows? What if the early-morning practice she was observing actually blocked her pathway to the Well? What if the walk that served others adequately did not match her pace?

Christ invites each of us to respond to God out of the uniqueness of our own being. Perhaps Pat was created to take a different pathway to meet Christ at the Well. Maybe in that evening time of love, creativity, and clarity, God was inviting Pat to explore a more direct path to the Well to find a deeper relationship with Christ. When we begin to attend our longing for God, it most often leads us to the path.

With these possibilities in mind, Pat's spiritual director asked her if she would try an experiment. First, she suggested that Pat abandon her attempt at morning prayer. Instead, she invited her to continue to settle into her evening time, but to intentionally infuse it with prayer. She suggested that as Pat entered her bedroom, she invite Christ to accompany her into the evening time. In Pat's review of her day, her guide encouraged her to ask Christ to consider with her the day's events, encounters, feelings, and thoughts.

Pat's spiritual guide thought it might be wise for her to ask these questions: What blessings did these encounters hold for me? What difficulties did these relationships hold for me? What opportunities or challenges has God offered me in this day? She affirmed the value of Pat's writing down her reflections, but suggested that they flow from a time of intentional companionship with Christ.

Both Pat and her spiritual companion knew that Christ was already in the evening time, that it was a matter of consciously acknowledging him. By making a few changes, Pat transformed her time of reflection into an evening prayer, complete with journaling. She quickly recognized that by establishing her original evening time of reflection, she had in fact found her way to the Well. She had actually begun this journey unawares. When she set out to pray in a pattern incongruent with her life, she found nothing but stark scenery and steep, stony trails. But now, by infusing her evening reflection time with prayer, she saw how Christ was drawing her along a verdant garden pathway, replete with fruits that challenged her spirit and refreshed her soul.

In summary, Pat's experience reveals at least two truths about finding your own pathway to the Well. First, the pathway always starts in the life you are living. The temptation is to look beyond yourself, beyond your life, to find the path. But you need look no further than the simple stuff of an ordinary day. There is, after all, nothing else for you to work with! You cannot live a life that is not yours. Once you begin the journey to the Well, the life you have will grow into something new. In fact, it may become entirely different. But the first step on the journey is hidden in the life you are living now. Look around. Explore the details of your days, and perhaps you will find a place to begin. A spiritual guide can help you search for the place or moment in your life where Christ is already inviting you to the pathway. But how will you recognize that sacred place or moment? The second truth gives us an answer to this question.

Your longing will point you down the path. Of course, it is not always easy to find the place or the moment that moves you down the pathway to the Well. You may not know what to look for. You may not recognize the pathway even when you are on it. So it helps to recall a moment in your life when you had a taste of the Well's water, even though you may not have recognized it at the time. This point cannot be overemphasized: If you can pay attention to what awakens your longing, you may have the best clue to your own pathway to the Well.

Examine your life as it is now. What makes you yearn to be loved and to give love? What captures your longing for freedom both for yourself and for others? What feeds your desire for healing and wholeness in your life and the life of the world? And how do you explain your constant attraction to creativity and compassion? Perhaps there is a moment in your week that draws you to these places in the soul. Perhaps a place — a sanctuary or a grove of trees or a section of the inner city — attracts you. Perhaps you feel most alive when you are visiting folks in the hospital or serving in a shelter for the homeless or writing letters on behalf of those whose rights have been violated.

No matter what that particular place or moment is for you, attend it in a new way. What blessings do you find there? What difficulties does it raise for you? What is God offering you through it? Invite Christ to go there with you. Infuse that place or time with prayer. Let it become the spiritual practice that sends you on the pathway to the Well.

If you take the first step on the pathway, you will eventually find a way to embrace other spiritual practices and disciplines — even the ones that now seem difficult and out of reach for you. Whether or not you develop these practices perfectly does not matter. What matters is that you continue to follow your longing for God — a longing carried by Jesus' life of transformative compassion, freedom, and love. Following the path leads you more deeply into the life of Jesus. You are following your longing and drinking more deeply from the Well that Jesus drank from.

A Visit to the Well

When our souls are weary and we find it hard to slow down long enough to take stock, help often comes from the outside. One form of help arises in focused or directed meditation. When our minds are distracted by countless competing thoughts, a directed meditation not only relieves us of the task of guiding our own thoughts but also points us in a particular direction. Understanding the difficulty of getting focused, we offer you the following meditation as one way to proceed to the Well.

A few words of guidance may prove helpful. The directed meditation aims to assist you in getting your mind clear, focusing your awareness, and presenting yourself to God. Keep your aim of entering the Divine Presence clearly in mind.

Place the meditation before you. Read the first short paragraph, pause, and follow the suggestions. Your imagination will enhance and amplify the directions. Continue the process of reading, pausing, and meditating, but don't feel compelled to finish all the steps. Remember that your aim is to be before God, not to complete the meditation. When the Presence comes to consciousness, you may wish to stop proceeding through the suggested meditation. Why would you persist on a journey when you've arrived at your destination?

The Meditation

To begin your meditation, find a quiet, comfortable place. Get seated comfortably, take a few deep breaths, and relax. Intentionally slow your breathing, or tell each part of your body to relax, beginning with your toes and ascending to your nose. Continue until you feel your body is still. (Pause)

Imagine a beautiful valley with picturesque hills as a backdrop to the greenery all around you. Notice the arresting beauty of the hills, bursting with spring color whichever way you turn, and pay attention to the blooming flowers that surround you. Take deep breaths of the cool air. Feel it tingle in your nostrils. Listen to the faint sounds of birds chirping and the breeze blowing through the trees. (Pause)

As you look around, you discover that you are on an old farm that was abandoned decades ago. The barn has fallen down, and the once-majestic manor house shows signs of gross neglect. Weeds and briars have created undergrowth that makes passage to it difficult. What a sharp contrast with the beautiful flowers, the chirping birds, and the picturesque hills! (Pause)

Despite the risk of getting scratched or cut by thorns, you feel an irresistible urge to explore the weed-choked yard behind the rundown, decaying house. Knowing the danger of forging through the undergrowth, you pause to wonder why. Why the yearning to explore the old yard? Why the risk? Why now? (Pause)

Without answers to your questions, you cautiously make your way to the backyard of the decrepit house. As you carefully push back the brambles and forge through the thick grass, your foot strikes something solid. Upon investigating, you discover boards placed together in a manner that suggests they are hiding something or protecting something. Further investigation reveals that the boards conceal a Well. You pull back a few of the boards and find an old Well that has an aura of mystery about it. This enchanted old Well has been hidden for years beneath the boards that once framed it and supported the rope and pulley and bucket. What is in the Well? (Pause)

An air of wonderment hangs heavy in the springtime air. Overhead, the blue sky with its white, fluffy clouds softens the questions of the moment. You begin removing the remaining boards guarding the Well. As they shift, rocks and debris fall into the dark Well, and the sounds tell you they have struck water. Finally, when you have removed the last board, you kneel to peer into the Well. (Pause)

At first you see only an inky blackness. But as your eyes become accustomed to the tiny bit of light in the Well, you notice that the surface of the water appears disturbed by the falling debris. As you continue observing, the surface becomes smooth and, mirror-like, reflects the blue sky and white clouds above your head. You feel that there is something intriguing about the Well. How did you find it? What does it mean? Why does it hold such an attraction for you? (Pause)

You spread on the ground the light raincoat that you wore in the cool morning. You lie down on the coat and peer deeply into the Well. Instead of sky, you see your own face reflected in the water, and as you continue to stare at the water, you glimpse scenes from your broken

131

relationships. You also see in that face the lines of fatigue etched there by rushing from one task to another. The face you see is frazzled, frightened, and weary. Suddenly on the surface of the water there appears a large heart with a huge black hole in it. What does the hole mean? Why does it appear so dark? (Pause)

Inexplicably, you find yourself drawn into the Well. On the side of the well you spot an old metal ladder descending into the depths of the Well. You discover it still has the strength to hold your weight. Down, down, down you climb until you reach the water. At first you hesitate, but then you ease gently into the pool of fresh water — all the way in. (Pause)

How remarkably safe you feel. All anxiety flees. The water is clear and still, no longer disturbed either by the debris or by your entry into the Well. You cup your hands and taste the cool water. You are immersed in the water, and the water is in you. Filling, refreshing, cleansing, healing, satisfying WATER. (Pause)

As you stand in the Well, you sense that you are one with the water, one with the sky, one with the blooming flowers, and one with the breeze. Just as you are considering leaving, the sun moves directly overhead, illuminating the Well and radiating its warmth into you. The sun, the Well, the water! What do they mean? Let yourself rest in the Well! (Pause)

Metaphor of metaphors, symbol of symbols, the Well, O God, is about depth, about life, and about You.

Hear my prayer: "Instruct me through your Spirit. Counsel me in the night. Show me the paths of life, and open to me your right hand filled with pleasures forevermore, that I may be a renewed faithful servant to you."

QUESTIONS FOR REFLECTION AND DISCUSSION

1. What does the Well represent for you?
2. What do you think hinders most people from seeking the Well?
3. What has most often been the Well of renewal for you?
4. What are the results of going to the Well?

SUGGESTIONS FOR JOURNALING

1. Spend half an hour with the meditation above, following each of the directions.
2. When you finish, sit quietly for a few minutes, then describe your experience of discovering and descending into the Well.

Chapter Nine

RESTING IN GOD

T he psalmist writes about "a dry and thirsty land where there is not water." What are the leaders of God's people to do when their wells run dry? Where will they find the refreshing drink that will give them the courage to persist? How will they determine when it is time to work, and when it is time to rest?

In our exploration of the spiritual life of leaders, we have strongly emphasized the importance of grappling with several important issues in the spiritual life of congregations. For example, we have examined the role of myth, the place of vision, the value of acts of discernment, and the importance of carefully examining the Scriptures. These and other suggestions we have made call for concentrated activity on the part of pastor and laity.

But there comes a time in our labors when we need to find respite. In one situation our need for rest will manifest itself as weariness; in another situation, as spiritual dryness. Sometimes we have done all that we can do, we have tried all the approaches available to us, and we are tired. At times like this we need to stop our efforts and rest; we need to trust in the goodness and faithfulness of God.

Lessons in Resting in God

When do we rest? What does it mean to rest in God? How do we cease from our labors and enter into God's rest? The story of one serious seeker gets at some of the answers to these questions. Listen to his story:

During a long stretch of years some time ago, God seemed far from me. But I was determined to sense God's touch again. In an effort to experience God anew, I decided to do *Lectio Divina* through the whole New Testament. I chose this as an ongoing way of focusing my life in God. I intended prayerfully to repeat and ponder and enter into a verse or two every week. I began at the beginning, with Matthew. Remember what Matthew starts with? I call it the "begattitudes": ". . . begat . . . who begat. . . ." The NRSV puts it this way: "An account of the genealogy of Jesus the Messiah, the son of David, the son of Abraham. Abraham was the father of Isaac, and Isaac the father of Jacob, and Jacob the father of Judah and his brothers, and Judah the father of Perez and Zerah by Tamar, and Perez the father of Hezron, and Hezron the father of Aram . . ." (Matt. 1:1-3). So, I began with the first verse.

All day each day of the first week I repeated the verse as I went about my routine. After the first week, my prayer was still rather dry. I wondered what this desert of a verse had to offer me. But I persisted. During the second week, I repeated the second verse hour by hour, day by day. Still no relief. At the end of that week, I noticed the smallest tip of doubt poking up its head. Was I wasting my time? Was I really resting with God or with a lifeless text? But I persisted. Third week, third verse: ". . . Jacob the father of Judah. . . ." Minute by minute, hour by hour, day by day, the week dragged on.

What in heaven's name was I doing with this deadly passage? How could I continue such a fruitless quest? Would chapter two never come? And what about the rest of the New Testament? I began to run my mind over the boring passages to come. How could I make it through them? But still I persisted.

Then I began my fourth week — first day, second day, third day — and suddenly it struck me: it was like I was being hit in the gut with a solid punch. I have a father and he had a father and he had a father. I have spent much of my life wishing that I had not had a father. I began to calculate how much of my life had been spent alienating myself from my father. These boring texts were now forcing me to face that truth.

I stopped *Lectio Divina* with the "begattitudes." I never got past the fourth verse. After those four verses I realized that I needed to take a different tack. In a retreat, in spiritual direction, and in therapy, I began to tackle my issues with my father. After months of serious work, I began to find healing.

I kept at the task of exploring my relationship with my dad for several years. I gained insights into myself, my relationship to my father, my relationship to my children, and my relationship to God. I practiced *Lectio Divina* with other parts of Scripture — those that seemed most fruitful at the time. Maybe it is now time for me to rest in God.

What is this story about? We are called to rest in God, to place ourselves in trust before God, open to whatever comes — springs or deserts, excitement or boredom, fruitfulness or barrenness. We will move from the desert to the spring and back again, as the person in this story describes. What we must continue to do is rest with God and trust in God.

As this story shows clearly, the Christian path will bring us times of thirst and hunger. The storyteller describes his decision to rest with God again and again when nothing seems to be happening in the relationship. He experiences only waiting, wondering, and a growing sense of frustration.

Across the ages, Christian writers have described times like this, when dryness fills all our attempts to receive God, when Scripture seems cold, when worship holds no appeal, when prayer offers nothing, when all the paths that used to lead to the Well lead only to empty cisterns. In these times God longs for us more than ever. In our moments of lostness, we are like the one sheep sought by the shepherd. Yet the sheep often does not know that the shepherd is searching. Only trust will sustain us through these times of waiting to be found — a trust that springs from our deepest desire for God and God's deepest desire for us. This trust keeps placing us before God even when the Scripture we pray seems to communicate nothing of God.

Such trust is visible in the description of the "dark night of the soul" given by St. John of the Cross. He describes a time when all the familiar paths to God seem to take him nowhere. None of the ways he has approached God and experienced God's Presence in the past offer help. No effort brings him a sense of Divine Presence. It is as if God has left him to fend for himself.

But deep within him there still burns a longing that he calls the "living flame of love" for God. From this desire for God flows a subtle feeling of rightness about the path he is on. Beneath St. John's immediate feeling of being far from God there lies a deeper sense that God has not abandoned him. Indeed, God is calling him into darkness along a new, unfamiliar way. Because he trusts the God who leads into darkness, he follows as through a "dark wood." For a time his life is filled with soul-wrenching, disorienting struggles — imprisonment, beatings, illness, and rejection by his community. But even in the midst of all these troubles, he trusts in God. This deep trusting distinguishes the "dark night" experience from depression, in which there is a complete lack of a sense of purpose. St. John's dark night is grounded in a trust-filled, purposeful commitment to rest with God, no matter what comes. Eventually, St. John, like us, finds confirmation that God has been with him all along, keeping the flame of his desire alive. God has been reworking him, creating in him new capacities for a deeper intimacy with Christ.

When this kind of confirmation comes — in healing, revelation, understanding, a sense of love, or any of the other fruits of God's Presence — we may be tempted to become distracted by God's consolations, to forget that we are still called to rest in God. The man who tells his story above did not yield to this temptation. After the extended period of dryness in his practice of *Lectio Divina,* a breakthrough finally came. Suddenly he received a powerful Word and an undeniable call to healing. And he stayed the course: he explored that path for a number of years, and to great benefit. He kept resting with God, kept trusting that there was more to be found along the way.

This is not always the case. After a powerful and sustained time of enjoying the fruits of God's Presence, we may begin to overlook the Source of our abundance. We need to remember that resting and trusting are also for times of fruitfulness, when we are exploring, learning, and growing. St. John of the Cross and other great Christian spiritual writers warn us that the risks of deception and perversion are greater during periods of spiritual bliss. The satisfied soul can become lazy, apathetic, and caught up in enjoying God's gifts rather than in enjoying God. Sheep can get lost in lush fields as well as in desert places, oblivious to the way they have become fattened and slowed by an abundance of food. They graze unaware that they are fair game for the wolves that constantly circle the fields. But surely the

Shepherd has not forgotten. God keeps beckoning and inviting us to come to the Well and rest a while. God takes the long view. God knows that our lives will turn from desert to spring and back, again and again.

As a leader, where are you in your ministry? Have you become weary in well-doing? Have you sometimes taken on more than you could effectively handle? Perhaps this is a time for you to review your commitments and to discern how these match the time and the abilities you have. While you engage in this task, we offer you several resting modes of prayer that will draw you closer to God and refresh your spirit.

Resting Modes of Prayer

Contemplation: A Pathway

For almost two thousand years, Christians have tried to describe for one another what it is like to rest in God, to open to God in a simple, trusting posture — being present to the Presence. The great spiritual writers speak of this as the "contemplative way." Weary servants of Jesus Christ have found it a constant source of encouragement.

But what is this way? We touched on it when we described *Lectio Divina* in our discussion of feeding on the Word of God. As you recall, *Lectio Divina* of Scripture moves from reading *(lectio),* to repeating a portion of a passage (rumination), to meditation (mindful consideration of a passage and the issues it raises), to prayer to God *(oratio),* and finally, to contemplation *(contemplatio).*

Throughout the long history of Christianity, the word "contemplation" has been defined in many ways. One common element has seemed to find its way into all these definitions. This persistent element is a sense of resting with God, "being there" with God in a way that does not involve human effort. By comparison, meditation calls for mulling things over, intentionally considering what a Scripture passage may mean for our lives, making connections, and examining issues and situations. These movements all require effort. But in contemplation, we are caught up in God's Presence beyond our own efforts. In contemplation, we no longer try to pray because prayer is happening in us. In contemplation, we are no longer aware of ourselves or even that we are praying.

In fact, the earliest Christian writers call contemplative prayer "pure prayer." In the fifth century, John Cassian, the man responsible for introducing monasticism into the West, wrote that this kind of prayer "comes forth from a fiery mental intention through an ineffable rapture of the heart *(excessus cordis)* by means of an inexplicable burst of the spirit. Freed from all sensations and visible concerns, the mind pours itself out to God with unspeakable groans and sighs" (Rom. 8:26)."[1] Other writers call this "affective prayer" and "infused prayer," as opposed to "mental prayer," in which the mind considers the meaning of things prayed. Contemplative prayer also contrasts with "discursive prayer," in which the mind thinks of things to offer in prayer. Cassian says that only a very few *abbas* and *ammas* have come to this kind of effortless prayer. It consists of "unspeakable joy" and "inexpressible groans."

Clearly, Christians have found in contemplative prayer a profound taste of what it means to rest with God. As the great spiritual teachers have explored contemplative prayer, two main forms have arisen.

Those in the apophatic ("imageless") tradition describe being caught up in no-thing-ness, a prayer without images or words or the emotions we normally feel. One's experience of God deepens and expands as no-thing-ness increases. Experiencing this kind of prayer is like sinking into a still, dark pool. The pool is Christ, who fills the place where images and words and thoughts have previously been. In place of inner activity, the soul experiences a sustained sense of being present to, focused on, and filled with God. The Benedictine tradition, in its imageless use of *Lectio Divina,* embraced this apophatic prayer of contemplation.

On the other hand, those in the kataphatic ("with images") tradition describe contemplative prayer as being caught up in a growing fullness of images. The experience of God deepens as the imaginal world becomes richer. Entering this world is like being in a dream state in which we are not aware we are dreaming and are completely drawn into the images that move and multiply without our effort. Christ comes to us, fills us, and carries us through the emotions and thoughts evoked by the images within our prayer. The Ignatian tradition, in its image-filled use of *Lectio Divina,* developed the kataphatic prayer of contemplation.

1. Quoted in *The Foundations of Mysticism: Origins to the Fifth Century,* ed. Bernard McGinn (New York: Crossroad, 1994), p. 224.

Whether our prayer of contemplation is apophatic, kataphatic, or a mixture of both, it is contemplative in essence: we are resting with God, deeply trusting that God fully carries us. The contemplative way encourages receiving God, being receptive to God, rather than attempting to get God to hear what we have to say. It emphasizes paying attention, noticing how Christ is present, and savoring that Presence rather than marching blindly through the day in bondage to our routine.

The contemplative way also fosters listening for the wisdom around us rather than trying to convince others of our opinion. In the contemplative tradition, we pay attention to something because we want to savor it, become intimate with it. "In place of manipulating," says Henri Nouwen, the contemplative Christian practices being "receptive before the world . . . no longer grabs but caresses . . . no longer bites but kisses . . . no longer examines but admires."[2] Contemplatives do not push to find the right path, convinced that they know where it begins and what lies at the end. Rather, they wait and watch for the path to be revealed, and trust in the Mystery that comes.

The tendency is to think that the contemplative way, the way of resting with God, is only for those secluded in monasteries, not for people with jobs and families and everyday worries. Nothing could be further from the truth. The contemplative way lies at the heart of Christianity. It appears in every part of the faith.

The Reformed tradition holds to the contemplative path — though that path is often well-hidden. Indeed, some may wonder where we find the contemplative way in the Reformed tradition. The Reformed tradition emphasizes paying attention — paying attention to the way things are. Usually this has meant studying or analyzing things in the world in which we live — Scripture, society, theology, and human nature. Ideally, we attend these matters to learn about them or to change the way in which life has been structured. Sadly, we often seek to understand a matter thoroughly only in order to dissect it and master it. Sometimes we want to master it so that we can get it right — part of our effort to justify ourselves. At other times we master something so that we can use it to our advantage in discussions or disputes — again, trying to justify ourselves by lording it over others. But

2. Henri Nouwen, *Pray to Live: Thomas Merton: Contemplative Critic* (Notre Dame: Fides Publishers, 1972), p. 24.

these perversions of attentiveness need not be. Focusing on an issue in order to control it misses the essential reason for paying attention.

As we mentioned before, in the contemplative way we pay attention to something because we want to savor it and to become intimate with it. We gaze upon it to take it into ourselves, much like the new parent gazes upon the newborn baby. The father notices his child's tiny ears, eyes, and hands, loves them, and appreciates them as gifts from God. In appreciating them, he realizes he is appreciating God's Presence in and through this little one.

Calvin encouraged this kind of savoring attentiveness when he pointed to our manner of receiving the things of this world. We are to embrace them as God's gifts to us, intended for our benefit and for furthering God's love. We are to savor them and delight in them, for in them we will encounter God working for us. In fact, said Calvin, we will see God's active Presence all around us, in every part of creation, if we only pay attention. Accordingly, he pointed to thunderstorms as the most powerful expression of God's active Presence in the world. And he pointed to sexual union in marriage as the most profound expression of God's love. God is sovereign and ubiquitous. Pay attention, he urged, and you will encounter this Mystery, the God of Jesus.

The Reformed tradition further embraces the contemplative way when it emphasizes the importance of responding with gratitude to God's grace and gifts. Combining this gratitude with the Reformed penchant for studying things and paying attention produces what we call "attentive gratitude." This Reformed posture of gratitude mirrors what the mystics call the "gaze of appreciation." Attentive gratitude does not replace careful study or loving action. Rather, it grounds our compassion in God. It fosters the kind of loving wisdom that joins compassion and justice in the active form of faith that is visible throughout the Reformed tradition.

And finally, the heart of the contemplative way appears in Calvin's notion of *pietas,* his word for spirituality. Calvin believed that the life of piety is a matter of being "engrafted into Christ." As he explained, "We also, in turn, are said to be 'engrafted into him,' and to 'put on Christ'; for, as I have said, all that he possesses is nothing to us until we grow into one body with him."[3] Calvin elaborated further when he said, "Christ is

---

3. John Calvin, *The Institutes of the Christian Religion* (Philadelphia: Westminster Press, 1960), III, i, p. 1.

not outside us, but dwells within us. Not only does he cleave to us by an indivisible bond of fellowship, but with a wonderful communion, day by day, he grows more and more into one body with us, until he becomes completely one with us."[4]

To be "engrafted into Christ" is to be filled with the Presence of Christ, the Nourishing Vine. Our life flows from that Vine. This image of the vine shows us the heart of the contemplative way: we can rest in the intimate, abiding Presence of God. We can rest in God, caressed, carried, consumed with wonder, transported and filled beyond our own efforts. The Reformed tradition, true to the heart of the contemplative way, calls us to pay attention to God's intimate Presence. We are to appreciate the ways in which the Divine Presence comes to us, to savor the gifts it brings, to give thanks. As these become an increasingly vital part of our lives, we will gain a deeper and deeper sense of resting in God.

Of course, the path of resting with God is not easily taken — especially in ministry. People expect leaders to be problem-solvers, always ready with the right answer. They expect us to know exactly what the congregation should look like in two, five, or ten years down the road. And some members will often expect us to push the whole congregation down that road. They may even question our leadership if we invite them to pause long enough to discern God's work with them. Taking time for discernment will seem like a waste of time. After all, the world doesn't function like that. (Perhaps that is reason enough to try a different way!)

But make no mistake; resting with God does not result in a passive and ineffectual way. For from it flows the gifts of the Spirit. And if the church is to be renewed in our day, it will take God's intervention. Consider how often the transforming power of God has flowed out of the lives of the great Christian contemplatives. Francis of Assisi stripped himself of the ways of the world and led the church hierarchy to a new understanding of the faith. Teresa of Ávila founded two orders and traveled all over Europe, solving disputes in her communities and advising popes. Thomas Merton devoted his life to solitude, yet his writings have drawn millions to Christ; his autobiography has never been out of print.

The followers of the contemplative way emphasize that we cannot simply sit back and passively enjoy our prayers of contemplation; we must

4. Calvin, *The Institutes of the Christian Religion,* III, ii, p. 24.

142

become engaged. If we sink into passivity, we will be out of touch with God's purpose for our lives. For instance, Teresa of Ávila says that as our contemplative prayer becomes deeper and deeper, we need to turn our minds regularly to meditate on the concrete realities of the life of Jesus and their meaning for our lives.[5] And we need to act on what we discover, because discerning God's way, after all, requires a desire to follow the way that opens before us. We follow despite the fact that our discernment will always be imperfect. But we must always remember that all our analyses and all our actions will be but dust in the wind if they are not grounded in a deep and trusting rest in God.

Attending and Intending Prayer

How do we come to an abiding sense of resting in God? First and foremost, we hold the profound conviction that we can do nothing to guarantee such trust, such rest; it is a gift from God. Nevertheless, certain practices can help us become more receptive to this gift. We have described some of these in our discussion of pathways to the Well. Two more, however, deserve mention. In fact, they get us to the heart of what it means to rest with God. The first, the Jesus Prayer, focuses our *attention*. The second, Centering Prayer, focuses our *intention*.

Attending Prayer: The Jesus Prayer

Perhaps you know about the Jesus Prayer. It is a short, simple prayer that is repeated throughout the day. When obligations press heavily upon you, this prayer can get you through the challenges of a day and strengthen your spirit. Many leaders have found this prayer helpful when they have been unable to have a period of quiet at the beginning of their day. A young pastor in spiritual direction tells a personal story that illustrates well the practice of this form of prayer. This same story, with slight changes, could be told by scores of laypersons. Here is the young pastor's confession:

5. St. Teresa of Ávila, *The Interior Castle* (Garden City, N.Y.: Image Books, 1961).

143

I was becoming more and more desperate. I wanted God so much. But where could I find God? How should I proceed? I thought I kept hearing a call to be a pastor, but how could that be, since I felt God had abandoned me? Here I was in seminary with nothing but a hint of God. I began to think it wouldn't matter if I were dead. But to kill myself would take initiative on my part, so I spent my days walking around in a daze, depressed and anxious. I even stopped riding my bike for fear that I would "accidentally" turn in front of a car.

I went to see a psychologist. He decided I was afraid of dying in a war. There was no war at the time, not even a "conflict." . . . I stopped seeing him.

But something "spiritual" entered into my awareness. At the beginning of one of my desperate times, I heard of the Jesus Prayer. Not knowing the whole prayer, all I could recall was "Jesus Christ, Son of God, have mercy on me." Somehow this short prayer attracted me. These few words had for me the slight hint of God. I began praying it in my waking moments, and there was not an hour of the day that I did not repeat that prayer. It was my lifeline to God. It kept my attention focused. The simple words helped me attend to Christ. By some stroke of providence that prayer enabled the deepest part of me to pay attention to God. Like a magnet, it drew me to God. Praying the prayer repeatedly gave me the sense of being with God. Even when my mind could not agree that God even existed, I kept praying, and my conviction of God firmed up.

After several years of searching, the breakthrough came. . . . I had never stopped praying the Jesus Prayer. Looking back, I think it truly saved my life.

The Jesus Prayer comes to us as a gift of the Eastern Orthodox tradition. From its earliest versions the practice of *Lectio Divina* came into the Western church. The Jesus Prayer is more narrowly focused than *Lectio* because it always uses the same biblical words. The prayer is a combination of the pleas in Luke 18:38 and Luke 18:13. The first phrase — "Jesus, Son of David, have mercy on me!" — comes from the lips of a blind man outside the city of Jericho. Despite the discouragement and resistance of people standing between this man and Jesus, this sightless, helpless man kept crying out to the Savior.

The second plea comes from the story of the Pharisee and the publican. The Pharisee attended synagogue and in his prayer listed all his pious practices. When the religious zealot concluded his prayer, the publican prayed a simple, heartfelt prayer: "God, be merciful to me, a sinner!" The first plea comes from a helpless blind man and the second from a self-confessed sinner. Aren't we often like one or both of these men?

Across the ages, Christians have prayed many versions of this prayer. Perhaps the longest is this: "Lord Jesus Christ, son of the living God, have mercy on me, a sinner." One of the shorter versions is very simple: "Jesus Christ, have mercy."

The earliest Christians who prayed this prayer described it as a prayer of the "mind in the heart." This makes sense when we consider how the praying of the prayer changes over time.

In the beginning, your body prays the prayer. Your mouth repeats it as your mind concentrates on physically reciting it and the meaning of the words recited. Your body may be praying as you kneel or as you breathe in rhythm with the prayer, but neither is necessary. Of greater significance is the constant physical and mental attention you give to reciting and seeking the meaning of these words.

Eventually, after thousands of repetitions, perhaps over a number of years, you no longer repeat the words with your mouth, but your mind keeps praying the prayer. Again, your mental attention is the important thing. What you discover is that this attention comes more easily than it did in the beginning.

Finally comes a deeper prayer of the "mind in the heart." At this point you no longer consciously think the words of the prayer. Now your whole life prays the prayer, without your thinking about it. Or, perhaps more accurately, the prayer prays your life. Unconsciously, you focus your deepest attention — the attention of your entire life — on God. (If you desire to reach the deepest level of this prayer, it would be wise to have the guidance of a spiritual director, because it has an amazing power to bring one's dark side to the surface. It can uncover parts of ourselves that are fearful or threatening to us. A knowledgeable guide can help us face these parts of ourselves clearly and safely.)

But the Jesus Prayer is fruitful at whatever depth you pray it. Try it in its simplest form, simply repeating the words over and over. These words are not magical, but they can be very powerful. Following the lead of

Scripture, they use the name of Jesus in a simple way to keep your attention focused on the heart of faith: on Jesus, and on the gracious mercy that flows to us from him. The wonder of the prayer arises out of its power and simplicity. Just repeat it. All that the prayer requires is your attention.

Begin to imagine not only how this prayer can strengthen your life but also how it can enhance your work for Christ. For example, you may want to review the task of a committee and the plans it has made and then bring these plans into the prayer. Let this prayer help you attend to God, to rest in God when you feel the press of responsibilities.

Intending Prayer: Centering Prayer

Centering Prayer is a contemporary practice with roots in the ancient Desert tradition. Also called the Prayer of the Heart, this way of prayer, in one of its early forms, has been described clearly by the medieval author of *The Cloud of Unknowing*. Like the Jesus Prayer, Centering Prayer aims to draw us into God's pool of stillness. Unlike the Jesus Prayer, however, Centering Prayer asks us to turn our *intention* toward God rather than focus our *attention* on God or some aspect of God's nature. Emphasizing intention rather than attention may seem like splitting hairs. But be aware that these separate emphases engage entirely different parts of our inner lives. In fact, they may be important for us during different seasons of our lives. So how, specifically, are these two kinds of prayer different?

In the Jesus Prayer, we turn our awareness to God by focusing on something that reminds us of God's Presence or on what appears to be an indication of God's Presence, like the words of Jesus. We trust that as we turn our attention to these sacred words, attempting to see how they are meaningful to us, they will turn our deepest attention toward God.

In Centering Prayer, we are not focusing on what God is like because we are not focusing on God's attributes. Nor do we necessarily have any idea where God is. We intend to place ourselves at God's disposal by refusing to claim that God is at our disposal. Our prayer is shaped by our will, our intention, to be with the mysterious God of Jesus. We long for a direct encounter with the Holy, not with others' reports about God. In the Jesus Prayer we gaze into the Well. In Centering Prayer we keep placing ourselves before it.

146

Here is a simple version of Centering Prayer. First settle yourself into a comfortable position, then close your eyes. Be aware of the busyness of your mind, and begin to let go of the thoughts and images that occupy it. Gently replace them with a word you repeat again and again: "Emmanuel." Know that each time you repeat this word, it reminds you to be with God. When you notice outer distractions and inner busyness interfering with your intention, acknowledge them, let them pass, and gently say "Emmanuel" as a reminder of your intention to be before God. Continue this practice for at least ten minutes, savoring the moments of stillness that may arise, moments when the busyness of your mind and senses ceases. Close your time with the Lord's Prayer.

Notice that in this prayer you do not explore the word "Emmanuel" for its meaningfulness. For instance, you do not ask, "Where is 'God-with-us' in my life?" or "What is Emmanuel, 'God-with-us,' inviting me to be and do?" Nor do you simply repeat the word over and over in machine-gun fashion so that your attention can be focused nowhere but on the word. Instead, you use the sacred word more gently and more sparingly; you use it as a divine prompt to refocus your intention.

Father Thomas Keating uses the image of being in a boat on a river to describe this movement.[6] As you begin the prayer, he says, it is as if you leave the boat and enter the river. As you pray, you float deeper and deeper into the river, resting more and more fully in God. But occasionally you may find yourself no longer in the stillness of deep water. Instead, you may be bobbing on the surface, caught in the current, or even climbing back into the boat, unwittingly focused on inner and outer distractions. At that point, you begin to say the word, and the word helps you drop from the boat, from the surface, into the water again.

This movement within Centering Prayer — from intention to distraction to intention — mirrors the movements of the spiritual life in general. In Centering Prayer the sacred word reminds us of our intention to be open to God and helps us rest in God's Presence. Each time we enter into a spiritual practice in the midst of our daily routine, it is as if we are speaking a sacred word, dropping from the boat to sink into the pool of Divine Presence.

Those who commend Centering Prayer suggest that it be practiced at

6. Thomas Keating, *Intimacy with God* (New York: Crossroad, 1994), pp. 6-63.

least twice a day for ten minutes. You may find it a restful, gentle time with God, especially if you are so exhausted by life's demands that all you can sense of God's Presence is your own desire to be with God. John Calvin once wrote about the essence of Centering Prayer as our desire for God. In fact, this focused prayer describes the heart of all our longings to rest in God: "The highest perfection of the godly in this life is an earnest desire to make progress."[7] The desire to make progress leads us along numerous pathways of the Spirit, where we experience the God of everlasting newness.

What a comfort! Sometimes all we have is a desire to try. When prayer is dry, when disciplines are beyond our strength, when crankiness and frustration and fear set in, maybe all we can do is bring to God the desire-filled willingness, the intention to become the persons God yearns for us to be.

And perhaps in the end that is enough. God will fill the places we cannot reach. God will carry us where we cannot go. God asks only for our intention, the outflowing of our desire.

Entering into Rest

In the letter to the Hebrews, the author writes to believing people about entering into the rest of God. We learn about this rest in the opening pages of the Bible, where it says that after six days of creation, "God rested." We who are leaders in the church are invited to enter into the rest of God with these words: "Therefore, while the promise of entering his rest is still open, let us take care that none of you should seem to have failed to reach it. For indeed the good news came to us just as to them; but the message they heard did not benefit them, because they were not united by faith with those who listened" (Heb. 4:1-2).

Claim the pathways into rest we have discussed. After your prayers of discernment and your efforts to fulfill God's will, rest in God. In the act of resting, you will continue to trust God to do the work that God intends. And in trusting, you will have done your part.

7. John Calvin, *Commentaries*, vol. 21: *Commentary on the Epistle of Paul to the Ephesians* (Grand Rapids: Baker Book House, 1984), p. 261.

QUESTIONS FOR REFLECTION AND DISCUSSION

1. What is the meaning of "resting in God"?
2. What forms of prayer often lead us into rest?
3. What is the difference between "attending" and "intending" prayer?
4. How does "rest" empower pastors and lay leaders?

SUGGESTIONS FOR JOURNALING

1. Spend ten minutes emptying your mind, centering and focusing your awareness upon God. In a brief note describe to God how this experience affected you.
2. Focus upon God's great love for you. Write a paragraph by completing this sentence: "Dear God, when I pay attention to your love . . ."
3. Now look within yourself. Find your desire for God. Finish this sentence: "When I focus on my intention to be with you . . ."
4. Reflect on the difference between these three experiences and write down your thoughts.

Chapter Ten

SPIRITUAL LEADERSHIP
ON THE CUTTING EDGE

What does it mean for leaders to live courageously on the cutting edge of their lives and on the cutting edge of the church's life? A mature, spiritually sensitive woman shared with us an experience that we believe will help you to imagine yourselves on these cutting edges. She told us about attending a Lenten focus group in which the leader invited members of the group to examine their consciousness for the Presence of God. In an exercise designed to assist them in this undertaking, the leader gave each woman a terra-cotta garden pot in a brown paper bag. She also gave each woman a hammer.

Next she instructed each woman to smash the pot with the hammer and to remove the fragments from the bag. Then she asked all of them to contemplate the brokenness of their lives and the fragments of their lives (not necessarily meaning "fragmented lives") before God. She suggested that some might even notice the lack of awareness of the Presence in the fragments of life represented by the broken pieces. The leader under-scored the importance of discerning God's Presence, but she also gave the women permission to keep their discoveries to themselves. But the women did share what they discovered. In an unexpected way the evening resulted in a flood of confessions and celebrations of the graced moments in their lives.

One of the women in the group reflected on the experience and what she continued to learn from her fragments: "As I used my broken pot as a contemplative focus over the next several days, it spoke two things to me.

The largest fragment said, 'This is not about you,' a wildly humorous statement to someone who enjoys being unique and special. The smaller fragment that rested comfortably in the larger one said, 'I want to be on the cutting edge of a revolution.'"

It is amazing how contemporary metaphors speak so directly to both our personal need and the need of the church. This woman's experience recalls another pot in the hands of another potter, who smashed it in order to remake it. Do you recall this account?

> The word that came to Jeremiah from the LORD:
> "Come, go down to the potter's house, and there I will let you hear my words."
> So I went down to the potter's house, and there he was working at his wheel.
> The vessel he was making of clay was spoiled in the potter's hand, and he reworked it into another vessel, as seemed good to him.
> Then the word of the LORD came to me:
> Can I not do with you, O house of Israel, just as this potter has done? says the LORD. Just like the clay in the potter's hand, so are you in my hand, O house of Israel. (Jer. 18:1-6)

Come down to the Potter's house. Come down to the Lenten group, and I will cause you to hear my word. Maybe this metaphor of the "spoiled pot" applies as much to each of us as it did to Israel and the woman in the Lenten group. We are fascinated especially with the word spoken to her from the smaller fragment: "I want to be on the cutting edge of a revolution." Did it take a broken pot for her to hear that word? Will it take a broken pot for us to hear God's call? What does it mean for her or for us to be on "the cutting edge of a revolution"?

Let's take a closer look at this phrase. When we place the accent on "cutting," the image of cutting through something comes to mind — like a razor-sharp rotary cutter that cuts through several layers at once or cuts a long, straight line.

In the church, long-established practices like worship and initiation into the faith become ineffective when they are covered by layers of tradition that belong to another time and place. Certain patterns of decision-making or perhaps the story of the church have been around so long that they have developed excess layers. Like the accumulation of barnacles on a ship's hull, these excesses need to be scraped away. It is necessary to cut through the years of buildup around church tradition to get to the core practices of the church. In the core remains the essence of what the practice is meant to be, and a sharp cutting away of extraneous accretions can release the energy of the original.

"Cutting" also applies to our own lives. From time to time we need scissors or shears to prune away the excesses of our lives, like the acquisition of material goods or the pride of success. This cutting helps many of us to detach ourselves from misplaced affections.

When we shift the emphasis from "cutting" to "edge," the demand is for courage. On the edge we face danger, challenge, and adventure. From the edge we step into the darkness of the unknown. The transition from the known to the unknown always requires enormous courage because we lose our sense of direction and also our sense of control. As long as we follow the familiar, we know where we're going, and we can control our reactions and responses. When we lose familiar patterns or fear the loss of them, anxiety causes us to turn back from new challenges.

Living on the edge calls to mind a scientist who has pressed her experiments as far as her knowledge can take them, and now stands at the edge of the unknown, reaching and groping for insight. For an explorer, the edge may be a marked point that designates the end of previously explored territory; at that point he must decide whether to go on or turn back. The cutting edge for the software developer lies right before her. She knows a certain function can be achieved, but she doesn't yet know how to write the program, so she must stand on the edge of the known and discover the uncreated possibility. We also think that many preachers are on the cutting edge when they read the ancient text of Scripture and hear the voice of the Lord speaking to our time and place. Then the preacher dares to speak: "Thus says the Lord" — a cutting edge for all hearers.

But the broken pot of the original example spoke not only about the "cutting edge" but also about a "revolution." Is it true that the "cutting through" or "cutting away" at the edge of our experience leads to a revolution in the way we see the world and the way we function in it? Generally, the word "revolution" evokes images of armies, guns, and violence — but it need not. A revolution can also be quiet and gentle but as powerful as an insurrection. Perhaps the quiet revolution may be called "a condensed evolution."

Some changes have occurred slowly over the centuries, like the evolution of the human species or the role of women, but other changes have happened much more quickly and with seemingly less struggle. Take the cell phone, for instance. Ten years ago it was rare for someone to have such a phone in their car or their purse; today they seem to be everywhere. Whether you're walking down the street in Hong Kong, riding a camel in Egypt, or visiting a remote village in Uganda, you may see someone pull out a phone and begin conversing. What a revolution! And a quiet one — except when people are unaware that others are listening to their cell-phone conversations! This one technological advance has changed the world for millions of people.

When we as a church live on the cutting edge, we will become revolutionary in both posture and practice. As you have worked your way through this text on spirituality and leadership, have you felt some urge to move out of the safety of tradition, familiar language, and accustomed ways and practices to engage in the adventure? Are you willing to risk living "on the cutting edge of a revolution"?

Spiritual Revolutionaries

Spiritual revolutionaries seldom have realized the scope and far-reaching consequences of their actions. Did the person who invented the cell phone have any idea of the revolution it would begin? In the spiritual realm, leaders have often had a notion about the will or the leading of God, but no idea of the full and powerful effect their choices would have. At the outset the notion may not appear to have much potential for changing anything, but the visionary follows the dream, and changes materialize that result in a spiritual revolution.

When thinking of revolutionary changes growing from rather small decisions, remember the example of Abraham. Inspired by the Spirit, this Bedouin chief departed from family and friends and journeyed toward the land promised him. The only evidence this faithful soul had was a voice that spoke to him with such conviction that he could not resist pursuing its promise:

> Now the LORD said to Abram, "Go from your country and your kindred and your father's house to the land that I will show you. I will make of you a great nation, and I will bless you, and make your name great, so that you will be a blessing. I will bless those who bless you, and the one who curses you I will curse; and in you all the families of the earth shall be blessed."

> So Abram went, as the LORD had told him; and Lot went with him. Abram was seventy-five years old when he departed from Haran. (Gen. 12:1-4)

This small act of obedience, which probably looked foolish to those who observed it, materialized into a quiet revolution. The consequences of this quiet, revolutionary choice were the birth of a nation and the birth of a faith that has spread to the whole world. The birth of the Judeo-Christian faith depended upon the faithful action of one man who believed God had spoken to him.

Leaders of spiritual revolutions have generally been persons who have been willing to take great risks. Risk in a revolution comes from the fear engendered by the cutting edge, the act of cutting away years of acquired baggage or cutting through layers of social conditioning. Recall the experience of Peter at Joppa when he saw the vision and heard the voice:

> About noon the next day, . . . Peter went up on the roof to pray. He became hungry and wanted something to eat; and while it was being prepared, he fell into a trance. He saw the heaven opened and something like a large sheet coming down, being lowered to the ground by its four corners. In it were all kinds of four-footed creatures and reptiles and birds of the air. Then he heard a voice saying, "Get up, Peter; kill and eat." But Peter said, "By no means, Lord; for I have never eaten anything that is profane or unclean." The voice said to him again, a second time, "What God has made clean, you must not call profane." This happened three times, and the thing was suddenly taken up to heaven.

154

Now while Peter was greatly puzzled about what to make of the vision that he had seen, suddenly the men sent by Cornelius appeared. They were asking for Simon's house and were standing by the gate. They called out to ask whether Simon, who was called Peter, was staying there. While Peter was still thinking about the vision, the Spirit said to him, "Look, three men are searching for you. Now get up, go down, and go with them without hesitation; for I have sent them." So Peter went down to the men and said, "I am the one you are looking for; what is the reason for your coming?" (Acts 10:9-21)

Nothing short of the power of God could have convinced Peter, a Jew, to go to the home of Cornelius, a Gentile. All his life Peter had been taught that certain foods were kosher and others were unclean. To eat unclean food defiled the relationship with God, and cleansing had to be undertaken. Peter knew these rules to be accurate expressions of the will of God expressed in the Torah.

Now, on the rooftop in Joppa, the voice that he considered the voice of Christ told him to arise, kill, and eat food that all his life had been forbidden. This meant, in effect, eating the kind of food that Gentiles ate — and, by extension, associating with and preaching to Gentiles. How many layers of religious tradition did Peter have to cut through in order to go to Cornelius's house? How much social conditioning did he override in order to obey the voice that spoke to him?

The choice to go beyond the tradition and to ignore all that he had been taught about the way of God forced Peter to risk feeling that he had disobeyed the will of the Lord. He also faced the issue of rejection and even expulsion from the assembly of believers. This decision was indeed one of high risk. Peter's risk was precisely the kind of risk that leaders in the church face today — breaking with the past, making choices that can incur criticism, trying to modify or change people's worldview.

Sometimes leaders in a spiritual revolution face rejection, ostracism, and the loss of status. But none of these earthly consequences seems very significant when a person has heard the call of God. When the sense of being an instrument of God is compared with gaining the approval and applause of mere human beings, earthly reward pales in significance.

Saul of Tarsus is another biblical figure who became a revolutionary when he responded to deep inner convictions. He had excelled in upholding the Jewish faith, becoming well-known for persecuting and killing Christians, but then he had a personal encounter with Christ. The value of knowing Christ became more important to him than all his other achievements and even life itself. He wrote to the church at Philippi about his assessment of earthly gains versus knowing Jesus Christ:

> If anyone else has reason to be confident in the flesh, I have more: circumcised on the eighth day, a member of the people of Israel, of the tribe of Benjamin, a Hebrew born of Hebrews; as to the law, a Pharisee; as to zeal, a persecutor of the church; as to righteousness under the law, blameless. Yet whatever gains I had, these I have come to regard as loss because of Christ. More than that, I regard everything as loss because of the surpassing value of knowing Christ Jesus my Lord. For his sake I have suffered the loss of all things, and I regard them as rubbish, in order that I may gain Christ and be found in him, not having a righteousness of my own that comes from the law, but one that comes through faith in Christ, the righteousness from God based on faith. (Phil. 3:4b-9)

Paul, the reborn Saul, provides a model for all leaders. He lived not for the approval of his peers or the applause of the crowd but for Christ. No form of human recognition, religious merit, or family heritage held any worth in comparison to the knowledge of the Lord. Facing rejection and even persecution did not deter him from his mission to serve Christ. As his powerful example reminds us, human achievement and approval can never be the goal of the faithful leader of Christ's church.

A spiritual revolutionary must even face the threat of death as the cost of his obedience. Recall the experience of Moses when he confronted the burning bush in the desert:

> When the LORD saw that he had turned aside to see, God called to him out of the bush, "Moses, Moses!" And he said, "Here I am." Then he said, "Come no closer! Remove the sandals from your feet, for the place on which you are standing is holy ground." He said further, "I am the God of your father, the God of Abraham, the God

156

of Isaac, and the God of Jacob." And Moses hid his face, for he was afraid to look at God.

Then the LORD said, "I have observed the misery of my people who are in Egypt; I have heard their cry on account of their taskmasters. Indeed, I know their sufferings, and I have come down to deliver them from the Egyptians, and to bring them up out of that land to a good and broad land, a land flowing with milk and honey, to the country of the Canaanites, the Hittites, the Amorites, the Perizzites, the Hivites, and the Jebusites. The cry of the Israelites has now come to me; I have also seen how the Egyptians oppress them. So come, I will send you to Pharaoh to bring my people, the Israelites, out of Egypt." (Exod. 3:4-10)

We all remember the events leading up to this encounter. Moses had fled from Egypt, fearing for his life because he had killed an Egyptian who was fighting with an Israelite. Years later, while tending sheep on a mountain, he had a strange experience. A bush was in flames but was not consumed by the fire. Noticing this phenomenon, Moses walked over for a closer look. From the bush a voice spoke, calling his name.

Once the Lord got his attention, the Lord called Moses to go back to Egypt and deliver the Israelites. No argument, no excuse, and no changing God's mind! Moses was called to deliver God's people, to risk losing his life in this act of obedience. Moses followed the call, and God faithfully delivered the people.

These notable models of faithfulness do not exhaust the list of those who have been spiritual revolutionaries among the people of God. The writer of the letter to the Hebrews reminds us that these four were not the only ones who were daring adherents to the call of God:

And what more should I say? For time would fail me to tell of Gideon, Barak, Samson, Jephthah, of David and Samuel and the prophets — who through faith conquered kingdoms, administered justice, obtained promises, shut the mouths of lions, quenched raging fire, escaped the edge of the sword, won strength out of weakness, became mighty in war, put foreign armies to flight. Women received their dead by resurrection. Others were tortured, refusing to accept release, in order to obtain a better resurrection. Others suffered mocking and flogging, and even chains and imprisonment. They were stoned to death, they were sawn in two, they were killed by the sword; they went about in skins of sheep and goats, destitute, persecuted, tormented — of whom the world was not worthy. They wandered in deserts and mountains, and in caves and holes in the ground. (11:32-38)

We would also add that the cadre of revolutionaries cannot be limited to those mentioned in Holy Scripture. Did John Wesley and John Calvin imagine the extent of their influence? They could never have known that the warm heart and the enlightened mind would initiate a revolution in Christendom.

We should also add to the list the spiritual revolutionaries of the fourth century. They resisted the enculturation of the church by going to the deserts of Egypt, Palestine, and Syria. They opted out of a culture that threatened to engulf the young church and tame its witness. By going to the deserts, these faithful men and women sought not only their own salvation but that of the church.

These brave followers of Christ may also serve as the best examples of relinquishment and abandonment. Like Paul, who relinquished everything for the sake of Christ, these saints narrowed their focus to prayer and worship. But isn't it also true that in some sense William Carey, the first modern missionary, and all those who came after him serve as examples of abandonment?

When we review the long list of the faithful, we realize that it was not only Paul and Polycarp who died for the faith, but thousands of unnamed martyrs, from the first century to the twentieth. For horrible visions of risk we need only recall El Salvador or Indonesia or South Africa. Perhaps the best-known spiritual revolutionary in America organized boycotts, planned demonstrations, and marched from Selma to Montgomery. Finally he lost his life through the misguided intention of a madman.

These references to spiritual revolutionaries remind us of valiant men and women in perilous times. Perhaps we have a tendency to minimize the threats to the church in North America and to its role in society. But the threats are real, and the risks of change and renewal are equally great. We are convinced that no amount of downsizing and re-organizing can cure the serious problems facing mainline denominations. More than anything else, we need spiritually alive and passionately committed leaders in our churches, leaders who are living on the cutting edge.

Cutting-Edge Issues

As we consider the critical issues facing the church today, it will be helpful to briefly revisit the issues that we have explored in the preceding chapters.

I

One of the cutting-edge issues of the church today — and perhaps of our own lives also — is the need for a clear focus on spiritual formation. For decades the church has settled for being an institution that emphasizes budgets, organization, structure, management, and an arm's-length relationship to God. To live on the cutting edge would challenge us to cut through this impersonal organizational superstructure to expose the core of the church, where we would again discover the Spirit.

Recognition of the Spirit at the center of the church's life and ministry would not only reshape our understanding of the church but also challenge our ways of doing ministry. In most of our congregations it would indeed be cutting edge to have clergy and lay leaders talk with each other about the living Presence of God at the center of the church. Even more daring would be setting aside time to share in serious, extended prayer together for the rebirth of the church.

In this extended encounter, perhaps the pastor and the elders could once again speak in Christian terms, unafraid to use the language of the faith in the presence of each other. Dealing with the faith at such close range might even call forth vulnerability from both parties. In this environment of openness, they might be pleasantly surprised by the manifestation of Divine Love and Power in their midst. Would this, perhaps, be the cutting edge of a spiritual revolution?

II

A spiritual revolution demands a spirituality of action coupled with a spirituality of contemplation. To focus exclusively on the spirituality of the angles — prayer, Scripture, and spiritual direction — will not bring about a revolution, nor will a singular focus on the lines — congregational care, preaching and teaching, and administration. Choosing one of these over the other cannot renew the church, as Eugene Peterson points out; each must inform the other. Yet it seems that we yield to one of two temptations: either we focus on Christian activism without giving due attention to the spiritual depth of our actions, or we focus on spiritual life without a corresponding emphasis on the tasks performed.

For us, being on the cutting edge would mean paying attention to the spiritual depth of caring, preaching, and administration as an incarnational form of Christ. With this focus, we become the eyes, ears, and hands of Christ when we engage in congregational care. With this focus, the act of preaching and teaching affords leaders an opportunity to become the voice of Christ, and the official meetings of the church provide opportunities for discernment. When leaders recognize that Christ is the head of the Church and that he leads the churches, a spiritual revolution has already begun.

III

Most leaders do not need to be convinced of the centrality and the authority of the Word of God in a vital spirituality. You have perhaps heard these affirmations of Scripture for a long time, so there is nothing too "cutting edge" about a strong emphasis on a biblically based spirituality. Yet, for leaders to read the text and listen for God to speak here and now may be new.

When the Holy Scriptures serve as more than a source for sermons, fires of awakening begin to burn. We have shown how Enlightenment methods of biblical interpretation have led to treating Scripture primarily as an object to be dissected and analyzed. Being on the cutting edge means receiving from these ancient texts a word from God for today. Imagine what might happen in this shared ministry when pastor and lay

160

leaders listen together for God's voice in the texts! Hasn't such holy listening created other revolutions?

IV

Perhaps it never occurred to you to think of the word "myth" in relation to spirituality. Yet a powerful myth, out of which your congregation finds its identity, makes its decisions, and shapes its life, generally functions beneath the congregation's awareness. If it is a myth friendly to spirituality, it supports the work of spiritual leaders. In a healthy congregation, knowing the positive myth enables leaders to work with it, thus making it a great ally. But if the prevailing myth is hostile to spirituality, it works destruction. A myth that does not support a strong spiritual emphasis blocks efforts to help the congregation respond to the call of God.

Nothing could be more liberating to a congregation than to have courageous leaders expose the hostile myth and its hampering effects. But, quite honestly, few decisions are more dangerous than the decision to expose the myth in an unhealthy congregation. In such a community, certain groups have a heavy investment in keeping the myth hidden, thus guaranteeing the status quo and their retention of power. Still, we believe this is a risk well worth taking.

Uncovering the myth is a cutting-edge move because it allows leaders to discover its nature. Working with the myth also allows leaders to have greater input in reshaping this guiding story. We believe it would be a courageous act for the leaders of every church to discover and discuss the myth driving their particular church.

V

If a congregation has a vision, that will have a powerful effect on its life. Unlike the myth of the congregation, which can function powerfully even if members are not consciously aware of it, the vision, to be effective, must be known, articulated, and embraced repeatedly. Yet the directional vision seems vulnerable to neglect, distortion, and obsolescence.

Seeking out a vision for a congregation qualifies as a cutting-edge endeavor because it stands in sharp contrast to managing a church only through goals and objectives, without a sense of the Spirit's presence and guidance. Management without the Spirit places control in the hands of the planners, whereas the authority in the vision originates in God. To say that church managers seek to plan something good for God and that vision-seekers aim to find God's will probably sets these two approaches in too sharp a contrast, but the distinction points in the direction we intend.

It is certainly true that leaders may become architects of very lofty and effective plans that achieve enormous good. Their effective ministry should not be discounted. We would never claim that God is absent from their planning.

Nevertheless, we are convinced that spiritual renewal will come in the church when our visions possess us rather than when we possess our visions. The visionary can never become detached from the vision and yet can never wield control over it. This highly challenging position puts the visionary on the cutting edge of God's intention for the church and in a posture of continual dependence on God. This is indeed a cutting-edge position!

VI

Like uncovering myth and seeking out a vision, practicing discernment cuts to the core of a managed and controlled congregation. Myth, planning, and management provide those in power with the apparatus they need to control the decisions and direction of the church. The myth exerts unconscious influence and direction with which the keepers of the myth are content. Planning offers a tool to maintain the values of the myth. Management offers an instrument to keep the plan on track and to safeguard control. All these tools maintain the "business as usual" church with its focus on sameness, safety, and conformity.

Discernment as a style of leading results in a 180-degree shift. Unlike the self-preserving institution that believes it must carry on the work of Christ in its own wisdom, a church guided by discernment asks first, "What does God call us to do?" Discernment does indeed presuppose that God engages us in the community of faith. God speaks to us, calls us, and directs us. Leadership through discernment depends upon recognizing the immediate guidance of the Spirit.

With other spiritual leaders today, we believe that a shift in emphasis from management to discernment would transform the task of elected leaders into a deeply spiritual enterprise. But directing the church through discernment requires cutting-edge leadership.

VII

When leaders in the church begin to see themselves as spiritual companions of congregants and not as managers of an institution, the revolution will have reached its first goal. Many churches today seem to have ecclesial norms that correspond with cultural norms. Leaders who can function as spiritual companions can help their congregations shift their attention away from these norms and toward their uniqueness as a spiritual community and servant of God. To move in this direction, those congregations aiming at the cutting edge will begin to pay attention to the gifts, qualifications, and spiritual maturity of their leaders.

Of course, only persons with a high degree of spiritual maturity can give guidance to the church and to other persons on the journey. Spiritual maturity requires leaders to know the essence of the faith as it is expressed in the creeds and the Scriptures, but it also requires them to know the pathways of their own spiritual journey. Leaders with these qualifications will know how to walk with new Christians on their journeys, and they will delight in doing so. Cutting-edge leaders won't relegate this important work to the ordained clergy only.

When a congregation begins to develop leaders with these spiritual sensitivities, it can consider itself on the cutting edge. Do you as a leader aim to move in this direction?

VIII

We have suggested that the pathway to the Well has been overgrown with tall grass, weeds, and bramble and may be hard to discern. But, once we make our way to the Well, we find refreshment and renewal. And we return from the Well ready to engage the tasks to which God is calling us. The Well symbolizes the place to which we return again and again for

163

strength of body and soul, the place where we receive the energy to carry on.

When you as an individual or you as a leadership team stand on the cutting edges we have named, you will from time to time need fresh visions of God's goodness and mercy. It is not that you will cease believing in the unconditional love of God, but rather that your experience of it will dim and grow thin. At the Well, the faint outlines of this love will be traced over by God's exceeding graciousness, and you will return with conviction to offer your life again to serve in the revolution.

IX

At first glance, it would seem that the admonition to "rest in God" would stand at odds with the notion of being on "the cutting edge." This contradiction probably arises in our minds because we know so little about resting in God. Resting in God does indeed sharply contrast with the life of today's church, which is caught up in breathless activity. Most of us know very little about rest, and even less about rest in God.

We would be on a cutting edge if we ceased from our own work to hear God speak to us. Leaders who intentionally stop to listen for God are, by this very act, admitting that they do not know the direction or the way.

How refreshing, and how cutting edge it would be, to admit our ignorance. And, likewise, how renewing to cease from our ways and listen for God's ways!

Taking the Risks

Inviting you to live on the "cutting edge" may seem as strange as asking you to fly. The whole notion of being a revolutionary in the cadre of God's new leaders may not even have registered in your awareness before you read this book. But we hope you will consider what it would be like to "fly" in this new way, however impossible it may seem, to join the spiritual revolution in the church, however challenging it may seem. Revolutions begin when the conditions have become so oppressive that nothing less than insurrection will suffice.

Perhaps one woman's explanation of how she resisted old stereotypes and dared to move to the cutting edge of her life to participate in the revolution will give you a feel for the shift we're talking about. She tells this story:

A few summers ago my husband and I separated for two weeks principally because of my frustration and unhappiness with being a stereotypical wife and mother. I felt stuck in old roles, and my reactions were more than he could bear. Separating for a time seemed the most civil action to take.

I moved in with friends who, besides being wonderfully nurturing folks, have an amazing sense of adventure. One day they proposed we go down to the peninsula overlooking the Pacific and watch the people who were hang gliding (then a very new sport). As we chatted with one of the hang gliders, he asked if I'd like to try it. I said yes! My response was either absolutely inspired or insane, since I am deathly afraid of both heights and falling.

Without giving me any instruction or protective gear, he strapped the glider on me and walked me off a hundred-foot cliff. Like the person before and after me, I could have crashed, but instead I experienced the weightlessness of flying. I think I knew what it must feel like to be a bird. I was thrilled. In my excitement I pushed the handlebar away from me, thereby tipping up the nose of the hang glider and loosing lift. I fell the final ten feet to the beach, gathered up the hang glider, climbed up the cliff, and did it all over again.

For me the experience was more than hang gliding; it was a prophetic metaphor of my life. I saw in this experience a woman who had been oppressed by old roles and social arrangements take a major risk and survive. She not only survived — she was flying.

At the end of two weeks I returned home, enrolled in college, began a career, and never looked back. I am so grateful that I took the risk.

I have just celebrated my thirty-seventh wedding anniversary.

You may judge this woman's actions to be stupid or foolhardy. But her story illustrates our point exactly. Living on the cutting edge requires something new. It requires us to embrace fresh visions, contemplate life from a changed perspective, and step forward with breathtaking expectations. It requires us to explode old stereotypes, take risks, and try again when we fail — if we want to be free from those restraints that keep us from God's best.

We want to take the risks. We want to expect more than we can imagine. We want to live a new way with Christ. And we hope you do, too.

QUESTIONS FOR REFLECTION AND DISCUSSION

1. What does it mean to live and lead "on the cutting edge"?
2. Name and describe a few "cutting-edge" people who have influenced your life.
3. Discuss each of the cutting-edge issues as it applies to you and to your congregation.
4. What has been your experience when you have been pushed or chosen to be on the cutting edge?

SUGGESTIONS FOR JOURNALING

1. Make a list of the times that you've been on the cutting edge of life.
2. Write a short letter to God explaining how you felt in one of these situations. Choose one that was difficult at the time.
3. Name and describe to God the cutting-edge issue in your life today.
4. Do you want to learn to fly?

BIBLIOGRAPHY

The Art of Prayer: An Orthodox Anthology. Compiled by Igumen Chariton of Valamo. Translated by E. Kadloubovsky and E. M. Palmer. Edited by Timothy Ware. London: Faber & Faber Limited, 1966.

Calvin, John. *Institutes of the Christian Religion.* Edited by John T. McNeill. Philadelphia: Westminster Press, 1960.

Cloud of Unknowing. Edited by James Walsh. The Classics of Western Spirituality. New York: Paulist Press, 1981.

The Collected Works of St. John of the Cross. Translated by Kiern Kavanaugh and Otilio Rodriguez. Washington, D.C.: ICS Publications, 1991.

DelBene, Ron, with Herb Montgomery. *Breath of Life: Discovering Your Breath Prayer.* Minneapolis: Winston Press, 1981.

Dugan, Kathleen Margaret. *The Vision Quest of the Plains Indians: Its Spiritual Significance.* Lewiston, N.Y.: The Edwin Mellen Press, 1985.

Farnham, Suzanne G., et al. *Listening Hearts: Discerning Call in Community.* Harrisburg, Pa.: Morehouse Publishing, 1991.

Guenther, Margaret. *Holy Listening: The Art of Spiritual Direction.* Boston: Cowley Publications, 1992.

Ignatius of Loyola. *Spiritual Exercises and Selected Works.* Edited by George E. Ganss. The Classics of Western Spirituality. New York: Paulist Press, 1991.

Johnson, Ben Campbell. *Discerning God's Will.* Decatur, Ga.: CTS Press, 1999.

————. *Living before God: Deepening Our Sense of the Divine Presence.* Grand Rapids: William B. Eerdmans, 2000.

————. *New Day/New Church.* Decatur, Ga.: CTS Press, 1995.

————. *Ninety-five Theses for the Church Today.* Decatur, Ga.: CTS Press, 1995.

Johnson, Ben Campbell, and Glenn McDonald. *Imagining a Church in the Spirit: A Task for Mainline Congregations.* Grand Rapids: William B. Eerdmans, 1999.

Judy, Dwight H. *Embracing God: Praying with Teresa of Avila.* New York: Abingdon, 1996.

Keating, Thomas. *Intimacy with God.* New York: Crossroad, 1994.

McGinn, Bernard. *The Presence of God: A History of Western Christian Mysticism.* 5 vols. New York: Crossroad, 1991–.

McKinney, Mary Benet, O.S.B. *Sharing Wisdom: A Process for Group Decision Making.* Allen, Tex.: Tabor Publishing, 1987.

Mead, Loren B. *The Once and Future Church.* Washington, D.C.: The Alban Institute, Inc., 1991.

Nouwen, Henri J. *Pray to Live: Thomas Merton: Contemplative Critic.* Notre Dame: Fides Publishers, 1972.

Origen. Edited by Rowan Greer. New York: Paulist Press, 1979.

Peterson, Eugene. *Working the Angles: The Shape of Pastoral Integrity.* Grand Rapids: William B. Eerdmans, 1987.

Purves, Andrew. *The Search for Compassion.* Louisville: Westminster John Knox Press, 1989.

Robinson, Edward. *The Original Vision: A Study of the Religious Experience of Childhood.* New York: Seabury, 1983.

Telford, George. *Monday Morning.* June 1991.

Teresa of Ávila. *The Interior Castle.* The Classics of Western Spirituality. Garden City, N.Y.: Image Books, 1961.

Ulanov, Ann and Barry. *Primary Speech: A Psychology of Prayer.* Atlanta: John Knox Press, 1982.

Willard, Dallas. *In Search of Guidance: Developing a Conversational Relationship with God.* Grand Rapids: Zondervan Publishing House, 1993.

Wuellner, Flora Slosson. *Prayer and Our Bodies.* Nashville: Upper Room, 1987.